i

Letters from the Gardeners Cottage Volume 2

SL SOURWINE

www.SLSourwine.com

To the two generations of robins that be-friended me during my time at the cottage. They brought me their mates, their young to feed, sang me songs in the glasshouse, and just hung out with me in the sunshine while I was having a glass of wine.
May I always be so lucky to have relationships with wild things.

CONTENTS

MAY 2020

The Gardeners Cottage
Argyll's Secret Coast
Scotland, UK

May 25, 2020

Greetings from Argyll's Secret Coast—which despite organising a marketing committee will remain as much of a secret this year as lockdown

Bluebells and sunset

in Scotland is not expected to really be eased until August. So a quieter than usual summer expected in a usually quiet place.

Our little area is responding largely well to all the changes honestly. I think in small towns a sense of community already exists quite strongly. Many of the local restaurants have started doing take away slots on particular days. But anything linked directly to tourism is shut down. The big spa/ hotel/marina is of course closed and all the big festival events cancelled. As many of you know for the last few months I have been helping out at the little gallery in Tighnabruaich. The owner and her husband are just the loveliest people who have a mission of bringing high quality contemporary art to rural Scotland. I really enjoyed the odd day in the gallery surrounded by the beautiful work and talking to people. In March we had decided to have me help out a bit more regularly. Then lockdown happened and the gallery closed. So instead of going in and manning the shop I have re-positioned my decades of marketing hat and have been helping them start on online presence and at least some attempt to sell work over the internet.

A handful of fresh sage.

A peony in the rain.

It's a lot of fun, and very gentle as the owner is not at all into tech! We're working on launching a digital event called the Secret Regatta at the beginning of June. It's in replacement of an exhibit that was supposed to happen co-inciding with the return of the beautifully crafted Fife sailing yachts to the Kyles of Bute. Instead it has become an exer-cise with older primary school children and local artists to capture the feelings of living somewhere where the sea has always played an important part. The artwork from the children will be sold alongside the professionals and all money raised from the sale of the children's work goes to buy art supplies for the two local schools participating! It's a wonderful little event and a lovely use of all these skills I built up over decades in horse racing. Wish us luck!

So many of you have been extra patient as the letters make their way to you. I can't thank you enough for allowing me to continue to send them even though our rhythms have gotten a bit off! I thank the postal service everywhere for their help in bringing these to you.

The First Year

It's officially been a year of Letters from the Gardeners Cottage! This is the 13th letter. When I started it I thought it would be something I would enjoy doing that would be a way to share what I was experiencing and maybe pay the internet bill each month. I had hoped to share a little of the peace and beauty that surrounded me in a way that shared the ethos of why I moved here: connection to nature, rest and pause, and reclaiming/rewilding parts of myself that had been overly in service to other things. It's turned into one of the most delightful things I have ever done. You are such an extraordinary group of people and I love interacting with you all so much. I love those of you who chat regularly on Instagram, or send me letters and Christmas cards. I love hearing about your life too. I love when you tell me that the letters have become a treasured moment of pause for you and where and how you read them. I love how many of you so generously subscribe for yourself and others. Thank you.

I want to give a very special recognition to the people who said yes to this little service right from the very beginning and are still here with us all today: Betsy, Kelly, Jacqueline, Brooks & Tracy, Susan, Ashley, Jennie, Barbara, and Joanne (my Mom <3). Your belief in this kept me writing and drawing and I can't thank you enough. This month 53 letters will go out all over the world and I am beyond grateful to all of you for your support.

I've been working on creating a collection of the first year of letters in a book format. I'd hoped to have that done, but like everything right now it is having a different idea about what is the right time for things. So stay tuned for that. I haven't really written yet what this full year has meant to me. All of the challenges, change, joy, and comfort this little spot on the wild west coast of Scotland has brought to me. Some things take a while to say I think.

The first Flag Iris.

A lemon blossom in the glasshouse.

Growing Season

I almost can't begin to do a report on what's growing because everything is growing so much! We had some long awaited rain last week and as the sun has returned everything has exploded. The level of green is as intense as it gets I think. It's so lush and absolutely stunning. I spend most of my walks moving very slowly along the deer paths. I love stomping down bracken to keep them open. It's basically put me on a rotation by day into my favourite parts of the estate as I attempt to keep nature from closing me out.

The bluebells still linger in the shady spots, but the little blue speedwell and the tall gorgeous foxglove will soon dominate. The first yellow flag iris was open the other day and when they are all open the ditches and burn-sides are awash with such a romantic yellow against the lushest green. The big thistles are opening and they always take my breath away.

The little creatures are growing too. Lots of goslings and ducklings trying to make it through the gauntlet of the first few weeks of life in the wild. I witnessed a huge gull steal a Canada Goose gosling right from behind its parents in the bay one morning. It was all very quick and hard to watch and hear. The parents kept calling for it and you could see them trying to decide whether to stay and see if they could get it back or whether to hurry the rest of the flock away. They haven't had the best luck and when I saw them today they were down to two youngsters. But they are big and healthy and I think gull as potential predator is at least off the table now.

Down the road a baby tawny owl fell out of a tree. It was rescued and brought to an neighbour to see what should be done. They fed it and took it back and found it a safe spot in the same tree. They watched it until the mother came back for it. I love imagining how that story is always going to be told in that owl family about the day it disappeared and went on an adventure with the giants. Closer to home, I was sitting on the patio outside the guest room the other day working on the envelopes quietly, Alfred sleeping on the grass across the drive. My neighbours and the kids came down and started telling me stories and chitchatting as loud as 4 year olds can and a big tawny owl made a bit of a fuss coming out of the tree beside us and flying away. I think we woke it up with our noise and it was not well pleased! I loved knowing that it had been so close, snoozy away while I worked though.

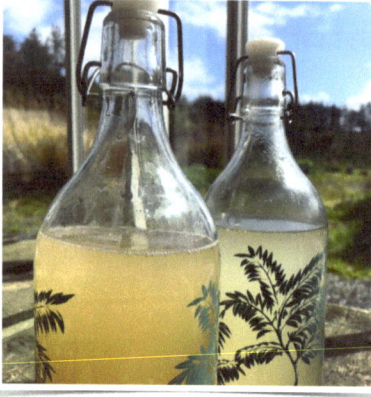

Ginger beer fermenting in the sunshine.

In the Glasshouse

This is my favourite part of everything right now. I'm sat in a lawn chair with my iPad perched on my legs as I type this to you. The glasshouse is just heaven. The grapevine has begun to fill in and has created a speckled shade on the eastern side. It is so warm and pleasant out here. It is my favourite place to sit. Alfred sleeps on the springy bits of the plant I've learned is called Baby's Tears or Mother of Thousands. It's a low springy, small leaved little carpet of a plant and I love it and give it free reign on the ground in here. The dream would be instead of this rough gravel floor to have some smooth stones to walk on surrounded by this lovely green carpet.

Everything in here is thriving. The jasmine has forgiven me for being so harsh with the choppers and has bloomed around the door. Its scent dominates the space in the loveliest way. I'm hoping that my new rose bush—The Poet's Wife, a beautiful yellow bush rose that was a gift this month—will take up the mantle once the jasmine finishes and perfume the space.

The food plants are coming on so well. I've already switched to salad greens from amongst the lettuce, kale, and beetroot leaves. My second batch of radishes put the first efforts to shame and are thriving. I (finally!!!) got cucumber seed to grow and will start my hope- to-be pickle crop in earnest this month. The tomato village is huge, flowering and I really can't bloody wait. Last summer's dietary staple of Spanish tomato bread for lunch is beckoning! I have some carrots and parsnip coming up in deep sandy buckets. I managed to get four butternut squash seeds to grow into seedlings and I hope they will take over the bottom shelf of the table underneath the grapes. My sweet corn experiment on the floor of the glasshouse went completely awry as I think a little vole wanders through here and bites them off (peas too). I'm trying what I am calling corn island in the middle of the floor in a container. I just really want enough to have even just one meal with barbecued corn on the cob!

Many of the containers I use in here are pieces of industrial plastic I've cleared from the beach. I've now got five fisherman's trays filled—they are perfect because they have both handles and drainage! I've also got a drum bottom (now corn island) and some more plastic crates. It feels really aligned with my imperfect attempts to consume less and not make unnecessary waste to be able to repurpose what would otherwise be in the sea. I'm even trying to make hanging planters out of old fisherman's floats, rope, and driftwood. I've got some herbs growing in my concept testing ones hanging from the roof of the glasshouse now!

I also have 30 celeriac plants that I have to construct some sort of defence for outside. Seriously what was I thinking?? I've planted 30 little lavender seedlings along the edge of the patio garden outside the guest room. I'm technically not supposed to do anything there, but it will be bloody lovely and I don't care.

Lavender was another surprising success from seed for me so I still have another 50 seedlings in the greenhouse which I need to find other guerrilla gardening locations for! The apricots and peaches are still doing wonderfully. I have managed to convince my little lemon tree to flower for me!

A porpoise skull discovery.

So I use the glasshouse for growing, as an office, as a fermenting room for my ginger beer experiments, herb drying, and a place to entertain my neighbours. My relationship with this beautiful space is really coming into its own this year. Sorry for so much detail! I have the beginners enthusiasm for growing food. I want to learn how to keep expanding my timeline about what I can produce for myself through out the year. It's a good start this year just to have so many lovely things on the go.

Animals and Archeology

A protected Scottish oyster.

I spent the last month deeply immersed again in looking at things which might be archaeologically important. I finally took the app What3Words and marked all the sites with notes. I've also been using it to mark hazel tree (cobnut) locations for later this year! I really don't know what to do yet with all the information I am collecting. But it just keeps showing itself in the landscape and I've found myself peeling back moss from fallen stones and marvelling at circular enclosures and more passageways carved into the rock. I'm sure I'll have a grand story about this some day. Just not this month.

One of my favourite unexplained stones carved with a corner angle.

Besides the saga of the gosling life here continues to be filled with nature. I had to chase a big red deer doe out of the garden the other night— we so need that gate put back! Their presence is palpable everyday in the tracks and poo that is everywhere here— even just outside the door and you wonder what on earth they were up to! I love to see them though. So big as almost to be almost elk-sized. I love

Interesting indentation or maybe warn cup marks.

watching them melt into trees or spring long-legged across the countryside.

There have been many toads about, one on the front porch and another in the glasshouse as resident stand out! But I bumped into two others secreting away from the birds in the long grasses of the edges of the lawn and in the garden rush grasses near the new raspberry.

The birds are really the stars of the show right now though. The skies and air full of their shapes and sounds. The swallows have returned to the nest above my desk window and there is endless swooping and diving as you make your way even around the house. The insects seem plentiful although the butterflies feel like they were waiting for that rain too. The buzzards and kites seem to be in perpetual argument with the jackdaws. We even saw a buzzard and a crane having an alter-cation the other day—but weren't there in time to see over what. Hilariously out my desk window one afternoon between the trees all of a sudden came this head tall enough to be seen over the stone wall, just doing it's bouncy walk down the road. It was a huge heron and we were both a little surprised when we made eye contact!

And just in case you are wondering poor Nigel the pheasant still lives! I caught sight of him yesterday and today and never has a pheasant been so beat up and had so few feathers. The fact that he might not be good at pheasant brawling doesn't bother me, but I sure admire him for being in the condition he is and not getting eaten by other predators! Seeing what I see on a daily basis—nests raided and broken eggshells everywhere (which Alfred now treats as canapés) if I was a pheasant hen you'd surely have to admire that a bit?

Until next month.

Much love,

Susie
xx

JUNE 2020

The Gardeners Cottage
Argyll's Secret Coast
Scotland, UK

June 24, 2020

Dear friends,

Where has the last month gone?

The sunset on Summer Solstice.

I feel like I've blinked the period between winter solstice and summer solstice. And yet the world has under gone monumental changes, I guess like it always does in this period, but this time it's also had our name on them. We've been so distanced and protected as modern humans in the west from the kind of change that nature rides through every year. I wonder

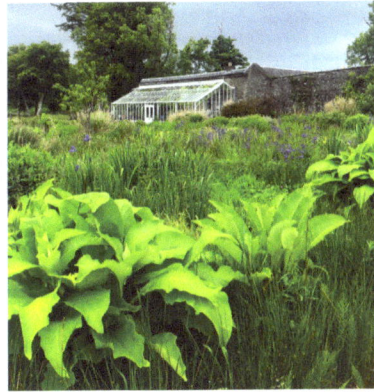

The wild walled garden looking back to the glasshouse.

if our forgetting how to be ok with that has exasperated our tendency to avoid painful topics or being wrong about things?

This is the first time I'm writing to you since the murder of George Floyd by a police officer in Minnesota sparked protest throughout the world calling attention to our need to dismantle the white supremacist system and the unwitting beliefs and training it imbeds in all of us. We have to do this work. I want to be clear about what side of this I land on so if you don't want to be here anymore because of it you are welcome to go. I'm going to write about this a bit this month before I get into the more usual topics.

I am anti-racist and as a white woman of course I am also racist! It is impossible for me to have been who I am and not be. That doesn't mean that I haven't had a ton of other unfair things happen to me, but the trials I have faced in the world have never been because of the colour of my skin. I don't want to live in a world where people aren't safe or thriving because of theirs. When we say things like we don't see colour, and everyone is the same, we negate and ignore the proven reality and pain of a great deal of our population. We need to look at colour for now, not because it actually indicates any value, but because we live in a system built on the assumption it does. We've got to replace that first. And we are going to make mistakes while we do it. We can learn how to do better and atone for them as we go.

Don't get me started about why statues of bad people are not what we should be fighting over. Take them down. Put them in a museum beside the roman artefacts featured in your stamps this month and explain the whole story. We need to care more about the lives of our neighbours than our ideas of the past. We can't change the past. We didn't commit the past wrongs. But we can't be silent about the harm done through colonialism and slavery still active in our world and of which some of us still enjoy the benefits of today. It's ok for it to be complicated.

We are in such a moment of opportunity to really get on with the work of dismantling the systemic racism that keeps black and brown people at a completely different level of disadvantage. (While we're stopping our destruction of the planet, pulling down the systems of patriarchy, and reshaping capitalism into something that serves instead of consumes too). All of this at the same time as COVID reminds us that we are still vulnerable biological beings and that it is affecting Black and Minority Ethnic communities disproportionately. It's a lot. There's a lot of work to do. It's time to rethink so much about the "normal" of our world and crack on with building something better.

Hedgehog neighbour in the twilight.

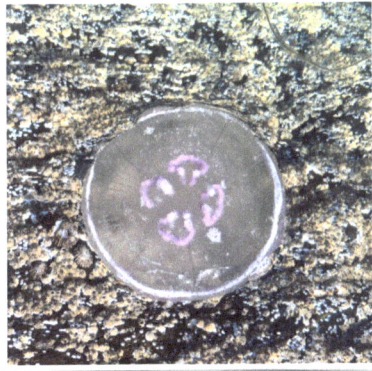

The harmless little jelly fish that are most common along the shore here.

When it comes to the things I love, and probably the things you are here with me for, like being with nature, gardening, walking... so many people are excluded or unsafe because of race. Not because they don't want to be outside, not because they have any less profound connection to nature and the land but because they are significantly less likely to have access to a garden, to have the money or means to travel out of the city, or to feel safe to be seen wandering the hillsides without the police being called! When I think of all the healing and strength that comes to me through the natural world I am heartbroken to have anything besides preference keep it from all of us.

One of the actions I am going to take to participate in the construction of a better world is that for every 10 Patreons I have each month I will be investing $10 onwards to people creating spaces that build connection and community in nature. As I struggled with cash flow in this last year of life-change I can tell you how much a regular commitment of even $10 a month means. I hope I thanked you enough for it. Now we'll also be doing this next layer of work and support together!

So far that means $40 per month and here are the organisations I've committed to and I can't wait to expand the list as we grow here.

Lemon Tree Trust (www.lemontreetrust.org) an international organisation that has a vision of bringing gardens and gardening initiatives to every refugee camp and communities of forced migrants in the world. They believe in the powers of gardening for mental health, women's empowerment, improving the environment and independent access to fresh food. They have the most amazing gardening competitions!

Soul Fire Farm (soulfirefarm.org) is a US based organisation which is committed to ending racism and injustice in the food system. They are a leading light on tackling equity on access to land and the systemic disconnection of communities of colour from the land. They raise and distribute food from their 80 acres in northern Wisconsin. They're doing brilliant work.

Land In Our Names (LION) is an organisation here in the UK seeking to uproot and disrupt systemic issues of land as they pertain to black people in Britain (food insecurity, health inequalities, environmental injustice and widespread disconnect from nature). They strive to creatively image a country where black people can feel at home in rural settings, delight in nature as equally as their white peers & be able to live off the land in ways which care for the soil, the surrounding biodiversity and themselves. I attended an online documentary film night they hosted this month and it was absolutely wonderful. I've donated to them via the Land Workers Alliance.

The wild swimmer in my favourite spot. You can see the stone dock just under the water behind me.

A still Loch Fyne on a hot day.

https://landworkersalli- ance.org.uk

I've got my eye on a wonderful project in Canada to start investing in for us from next month too. And I'm not a little excited about this! Your support of me and my writing project creates so much magic and connection already, thank you to all of you who write back or message via social media. I love it, and

I can't wait to see what else we are capable of doing together.

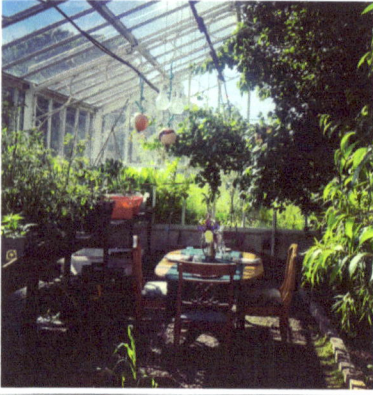

I threw my first dinner party in the glasshouse this month. It was for my neighbours Dara (4) and her brother Coran (2). It was a huge success particularly the Eton mess for dessert.

Beyond Midsummer

Mid-summer has come and passed. I was out with my dog Alfred last night at around 10:30pm and it's still only softening twilight. I find myself both staying up later and waking earlier which isn't the most useful combination! But mostly I drift back to sleep and wake when the birds are getting loud.

Fledgling season has been on full tilt. So many wobbly little fliers taking to the skies for the first time with lots of calls back to Mom and Dad as they go. It's amazing once you tune to it. I had a wee robin fly within an inch of my head and land on a branch beside me. It looked back at me a little bit in shock and reminded me of being on rollerblades in the park before you have any idea of how to stop—you just grab the first tree that's close enough! I watched a little family of wrens cheerfully peeping as they popped out of a nest I didn't know was just a few feet from the glasshouse door. They went exploring amongst the reeds of the little pond before attempting to fly its length. The baby swallows are still in the nest above my desk as I write, but I think it's only a matter of days. Then they'll fatten up on all the lovely bugs on offer before disappearing again on their journey back to Africa. Did you know that before they actually could follow the secret journeys of birds, it was thought swallows did everything from winter under the ice in the pond to hibernate deep in the mud!

This week has been a particularly fawn-filled week. On the solstice Alfred and I walked down to the beach by the standing stones for sunset. As we came over the hill I noticed a Roe deer doe coming out of the bracken. I made a noise to let her know we were there and grabbed Alfred before he saw her. I was so glad I did because twin fawns came out behind her all legs and surprise as they looked up at us then bounded off behind her. Then yesterday as I was headed out the drive a Red Deer fawn—so much bigger and bright red coat with spots just like they paint Bambi—had obviously been hidden away by mom in the little forest there. Not being that obedient it was up and moving about with a leaf hanging from its lips. So adorable!

I broke my phone by drowning it falling out of a kayak this month so I'm on an old phone with a broken camera at the moment! So my pictures won't include moments like that until I manage to get it replaced. I'll probably just start carrying my iPad because it's making me crazy not to be able to take spontaneous pictures for you!

My pledge to swim in the loch at least once a month for a whole year is easily fulfilled these days. It's been so warm and I find myself actually swimming and trying to reach new distances instead of just floating about until the cold sets in. It's become one of my favourite things I do so if you ever visit be prepared to try at least once! I also learned this month that the little jellyfish I see most often don't sting! Woo hoo! My favourite spot is off an old stone boat landing that has been abandoned. It's a perfect launch point.

In the Glasshouse & Garden

Bounty.

In all of the seriousness of the change happening in the outside world I also get to report a really wonderful development here on the estate. The manager that made things quite difficult for me here and even made me question to an extent whether or not I would be able to stay has quit! I didn't write of the bullying behaviour that has gone on after and around the legal dispute with the glasshouse, but it was pretty tough. The ridiculousness of it even got to the point where he barricaded the orchard so I could no longer get any apples and instead he threw barrels of them in the sea this spring! But it's over. He's gone and my lovely neighbours and I have begun the re-stewarding of the orchard. Happy days! Apple pie for everyone this fall!

It's wonderful to be able to get excited again about the old rhubarb that is there and the medlar trees whose fruit I was so looking forward to learning to process which last year were just left to rot. So look for more on all of that after the frost this autumn!

My favourite thing is happening right now in the glasshouse and that is the apricot harvest is starting. When things were difficult last year I seriously decided that no matter what happened I was making it through one more apricot harvest! And here I am and the world is indeed different.

My neighbour gave me a bottle of fancy brandy he was gifted and had never drank (just moved it from house to house) and so the apricot brandy should be extra good this year! He's also trying to convince me that we should try to make some wine from the grapes this year. I told him that with a surname like Sourwine my ancestors had probably demonstrated quite clearly that this was NOT our zone of genius. We'll see.

The Poet's Wife rose giving me such joy.

The sweet peas and the roses are bringing me so much flower joy at the moment. As you can tell by your envelope art! My new yellow rose smells divine and has taken over from the jasmine at scenting the glasshouse at the moment. Out on the estate the elder trees are all flowering and I've got the first batch of elderflower cordial made.

I hope you've managed to hold on to the beauty and plenty in your world this month too at the same time we figure out how to make a much better world for all of us.

Remember that rest and taking care of yourself is also a radical act. It gives us the energy and resources to tackle things that exhausted people just can't do.

I love you.

Susie
xx

"We have, I believe, a moral responsibility to do whatever we can to envisage new and different ways of being – and then to be those... What would it feel like if we got everything right?"
- Manda Scott, Accidental Gods Podcast

The Gardeners Cottage
Argyll's Secret Coast
Scotland, UK

July 24, 2020

Greetings friends!

I'm writing to you from the
kitchen while my first loaf of
bread is in the oven. It's a

One of our few sunny July days so far.

pleasant thing to do in the morning—all the work is done just a
little artistic effort with the scoring cuts on the top and popping it in the oven. I mostly keep the heat off as much as I can
in the summer so the toasty kitchen from baking for an hour or
so makes it a nice welcome into the day. My sourdough starter
is actually a year old this month! So Happy Birthday Ada! (I
named it after my grandmother's friend Ada who had big
strong arms you could imagine kneading dough for days).

Crimson bottlebrush representing the Australian readers in the garden! The bees love them and they are part of the myrtle family.

Blueberries not quite ready.

In the Glasshouse and Gardens

I've been thinking a lot about food this month. The kind I am growing. What it takes to feed myself for a season or a year. Noticing what I really eat and what I actually want to eat. This year with having so much more food on the go in the glasshouse I am really conscious of how inadequate it all is (besides tomatoes this year!) to actually feed myself. What am I growing that could keep for a winter? How can you preserve things without unending amounts of sugar? It's all such a relearning curve and I often wish I could talk to my grandmothers and great-grandmothers and hear about things that were forgotten. Don't get me wrong I'm not at all against innovation and things being easier to do. But some of the shortcuts we made haven't been incredibly healthy and leave us really vulnerable because we no longer know how to do it ourselves. I find things in fragments and like watching friends and family do a task and asking about it so I can learn or research.

It's some of the wisdom I'm interested in collecting and hopefully sharing once I figure it out!

Things are growing with the abundance of mid-summer. We're in that phase where you think it will never end and it's hard to remember winter's short days and naked trees. Everything is so fecund. There are a thousand shades of green interrupted by the purples of thistles and heather, and the yellows of wild flowers. We've been through the apricots and black currants now. The birds

Creme de Cassis

FROM PRACTICAL SELF RELIANCE BLOG

You will need:

2 cups black currants
750ml (about 3 cups Vodka)
1 cup of sugar
1 cinnamon stick
5-6 months steeping time.

Instructions:

Wash the fruit. Stemming is optional.
Put the currants, sugar, and cinnamon stick in a jar and fill up as much as you can with vodka.
Cover and store in a dark spot and shake whenever you remember.
Strain after 2 to 3 months and then let it mature for a couple of more.
Crack it to celebrate the new year!

cleared the cherries before I could get more than the first attempt at pie filling and a bowlful to eat. The peach tree has started throwing its fruit on the floor. I had my first one the other day and it was gorgeous. Then I tried to share with my neighbours and they weren't ripe! So the perfect time to pick a peach is a work in progress.

I've made the yummiest spicy black currant chutney and they have joined the apricots in the boozy adventures and I am attempting to make my own Creme de Cassis (Kir Royal) so Christmas and new year should taste festively of summer at the cottage. We're patiently waiting on the blueberries. I expect it will mostly just be standing around the bush and eating them going on. It will be hard to get the kids to try and save them just like the strawberries. And that's perfect too.

Life on the estate is settling into our new normal and the peacefulness of not having to be on guard all the time is such a relief. I've even felt confident enough to put some plants in the ground! I don't remember if I told you, but I started lavender plants this year and all of them germinated and grew much to my surprise! So I gave a lot away and I've managed to plant over 50 individual plants to help re-draw some edges around the outside of the cottage as well as on the section of the walled garden I was given to use. Ironically the little wasteland that I was assigned has turned out to be one section of the garden where the drainage isn't damaged. The fancy bit that the old manager claimed for himself is actually a mess that has rotted much of what was planted in it! So I'm working on getting my section cleared and planted for some winter vegetables I hope.

It was wonderful to see the return of the Cinnabar moth caterpillars to munch the ragweed on the estate. They pupate into the most beautiful bright red and black moths.

But the lavender is out there on the front edge soaking up the sun. I hope some of them flower this summer. It will be so joyful to see that result from seed. And it gives me future joy to imagine them flowering, scented, and filled with bees out there for a long time.

The Wild Things

The creatures too are taking in the abundance of summer as fast as they can. In the daylight stepping out into the courtyard of the cottage swallows swoop and chirp about your head. In the evening they are replaced by the beautiful little pippistrelle bats who fly almost exactly the same pattern, but silently. I love watching them. The little songbirds have gone to moult and it's usually quiet without them.

COMMON BUZZARD, *Buteo buteo*

An illustration of the Common Buzzard from Blandford's "Birds in Colour." Aren't they fierce and wonderful?

But this year the buzzards (a large bird of prey more similar to an eagle than the carrion eating buzzard in North America) have raised a family and their life-skills education has become the soundtrack of July. There are three youngsters, that I can tell, and they are so vocal! Where mom and dad just get on with the business of hunting, buzzards are deadly predators, the youngsters talk through it all! They tell each other what they are doing, who they've seen, if I come out of the house... it's wonderful. I've been recording them trying to capture how the air sounds filled with their joys. We also keep catching them having squirmishes with herons! The noise that generates calls you immediately to see what on earth is going on. I can't tell who wins or who wants what, but it's definitely an argument! The buzzard is a great conservation story. It was once in danger of disappearing entirely and through protections has been able to reestablish itself. It's illegal to hunt them and you can bet that I'll be watching them closely when they put the pheasant chicks out this year.

The thousands of little toads that hatched are still bopping about on the ground. There are always one or two trying to hop into the kitchen if I leave the door open! So funny. The neighbour children are always very happy to grab them and relocate them when their visit has given the opportunity.

On the Envelopes

The envelopes this month aren't my usual painting, but I didn't think you'd mind the slight variation for a chance to see the lay of the land around the cottage that I'm always talking about. The image that I chose is a selection from the very first edition of the Ordnance Survery Map for this area. The survey was conducted in 1865 and published in 1870. The Gardeners Cottage is on there in its current shape—I just drew it larger so you could see where.

There is also this interesting book called Ordnance Survey Name Books that goes along with the surveys and describes each of the place names, looks into the spellings and the meanings of the Gaelic words, as well as cites the sources and some interesting oral history facts alongside. It's absolutely amazing and all available on the internet with a little digging. Black Harbour (the bay by the standing stones) is recounted as well known and a haven for local fisherman in rough weather. I personally love maps so much—I'm looking forward to getting my globe collection up here to the cottage soon. Adding in this

new level of exploring them through time and people is just
wonderful. The Ordnance Survey Maps, for those not from the
UK, are the most remarkable works. They started in 1781 and
work to provide detailed local maps of every area of the UK.
They have footpaths for walking and ruins and Roman spots
and hills and parking. They are the absolute best resource and
one of the reasons it's so popular to take a walking holiday here
in the UK. Our local area hasn't been surveyed for a while so it's
interesting to get out and try to use the paths and it reminds
you what a gem these things are. I keep our local one on the
wall in the cottage for everyone (and me) to stare at.

Guests on the Way

As I write it's also the first time I'm preparing the cottage for
company in six months! Some dear friends are coming up from
London with their children and I'm so thrilled. I love the idea of
turning children loose here. I like taking them out and helping
them notice what's around them. Lots of plans for walks and
swims and bonfires on the beach. I paid more than you want to
imagine for some American style marshmallows for roasting on
the fire. It's going to be great.

I hope you too have the possibility of time with loved ones
and that you are well and feeling safe. This rollercoaster of life
right now is pretty intense. As I've said before I keep taking my
cues from nature. She's flowering and fruiting and growing
anyway, even though she knows that everything isn't the same
as it's been. I've also noticed she's in a bit of a hurry to get to
the good stuff this year too. So don't put off choices that make
you thrive right now. We are amazing creatures and we can
hold the hard stuff, do difficult things, take care of each other

and relish our joy too. It's something incredibly wonderful about being human. It doesn't have to be simple to be right.

Much love,

Susie
xx

Bats can hear shapes. Plants can eat light. Bees can dance maps. We can hold all these ideas at once and feel both heavy and weightless with the absurd beauty of it all.
- Jarod K Anderson

AUGUST 2020

The Gardeners Cottage
Argyll's Secret Coast
Scotland, UK

August 19, 2020

Hello dear ones! How are you?

I was more excited than usual to write to you this month for many reasons. I always have so much to tell you about what I'm learning or thinking and then in this verdant season of late summer everything is growing quickly and is basically keeping me enamoured of each and every plant and the wonder of what is being produced.

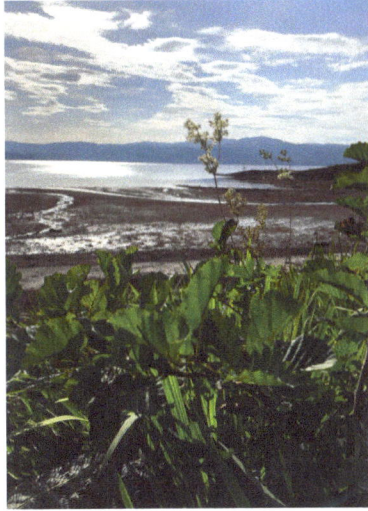

One of my favourite wild flowers, Meadowsweet, above Ardmarnock Bay. Meadowsweet has been used for pain relief and prized for its long lasting sweet scent. Elizabeth I apparently had fresh meadowsweet scattered amongst the rushes on the floor of her bedchamber.

August was full of love and fun and good company here at the Cottage. My dear friends from London with their young family arrived for a two week stay and the pace of life here went to match that of an energetic five year old boy and a 15 month old girl. But it was wonderful. My goal of modelling a modern reconnection to nature and radical rest as a creative force takes many shapes. And after months in lockdown in London it was so fun to remind the little one about being a bit wild in nature. It reminded me how fragile our relationship to the more than human world is and also how easily reignited.

So we caught frogs (really toads) and crabs, he climbed trees and played in the stream naked with the neighbour kids, learned to hold a chick and how to scramble around the coast—slow particular steps and keep off the seaweed! We went to Ostel Bay's big sandy beach just to make epic sandcastles and we had a BBQ on the beach at home with what might have been the largest marshmallows ever made! We had an amazing time and it was so good for me to live amongst a family for a while again.

Directly after that I was joined for a few days by a friend who is a professional cook that had been hired to look after a family at their estate further up in the Highlands for a couple of weeks. Becky arrived with a 'Tigger bounce' (as she says herself) and a car packed with goodies and proceeded to spoil me rotten with her cooking for a few more days. I introduced her to wild swimming— something she really only wanted the company to be brave enough to do—and we had one of the best swims I have had yet here. Every time I take someone swimming in the loch who has secretly longed for that type of experience—the way I did once too—it fills something in my heart that I can't even describe. I always text my friend Bridget who was the one to initiate me and we share the joy of passing it onwards. When was the last time you swam in a natural body of water?

And as the universe seems to like to reflect my life with nature— madly, wonderfully full of many things at this season—yesterday was also my 49th birthday. Entering into the last year of this particular decade of my life in this place and space in myself has been a complete gift. I have never felt more treasured and loved and excited about the future than I do right at this moment. So whether you smile fondly in reminiscence at my little milestone, or it is a number that seems far away and incomprehensible, I can tell you the secret to what I know in this moment that has made it all possible: I am finally learning how to treasure and trust myself. I've always been indescribably lucky in the people who love me. I was born into a big family. I have found soul friends at every stage and location of my life. They have all always been ridiculously generous, affectionate, and approving of me. Many of you

demonstrating that right now by being amongst the subscribers of these letters. But the truth is I never felt that way towards myself. I was the first to find fault or slam the brakes on a dream. I still do it. But this last year of my life in particular has been the most productive space to learn how to stop that. How to be more gentle with myself and believe in myself and my timing. Yes everything could be done faster or bigger or better or more true. But through prioritising my solitude and a focus on my relationship with myself, and myself as part of the natural world, I've manage to do what I couldn't do before.

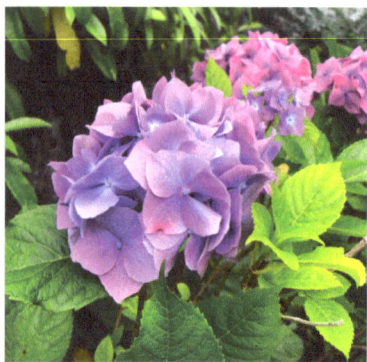

It seems fitting to have found myself in The Gardeners Cottage for this phase of my life. And as always the universe loves a play on words, because it is not the exterior I am most called upon to garden. And as I learn to let Nature heal herself around me I see that capability in myself too. So as I tend this new way of being with myself my goal is to be more of service to all of us trying to find our way "further in, farther up" as CS Lewis wrote, to deconstructing the things that no longer serve any of us and to help create (or at least not interfere with) a thriving planet both for humans and the more than human world. Thank you for being part of that with me. You've been the perfect wild swimming buddies.

In the Glasshouse and Gardens

If I attempted to share all the happenings I would over-take the letter! Everything is completely beautiful and shar-ing its bounty generously. I'll share my favourite pictures of the month. The tomatoes are all that I could have hoped and are giving me and my neighbours their sunny good-ness by the bowlful right now. My cucumbers currently have my heart though as I think I will get to make at least a couple of jars of my sister's amazing dill pickle recipe! They aren't as excited by dill pickles here in the UK so I can't wait to have some in stock. It will taste like my childhood home in my cup-board (Saskatchewan for me). For the first time I am working on my winter seedlings at the correct time! I have new beetroot, spinach, kale, and a second sowing of peas, yellow tomatoes to get us deep into autumn and even my pepper plants are thriving during the heat we've had.

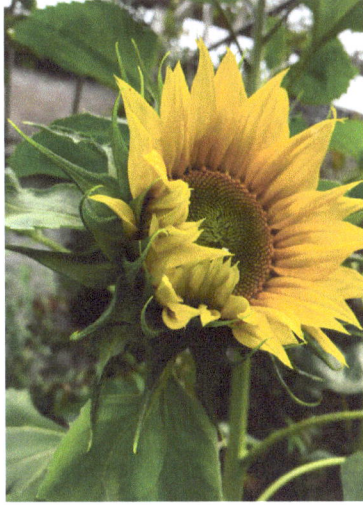

The grape crop this year, after last year's pruning, is in really good shape so far and the fruit is starting to turn. We are going to attempt to do the first Gardeners Cottage wine! It will probably be terrible, but tons of fun. While my friend Geordie was here I put him to work helping me prune the apricot tree. The top of the tree was beginning to push strongly against the top of the glasshouse and not only was it unmanageable up there it would also have done some long term damage. There is so much more light for the little peach tree beside it. It inspired me to get the peaches done yesterday too. It's all about the journey of getting them trained back against the wall. I enjoy the idea now that it's a multi-year endeavour to do it and work to preserve some crop in the next year too.

Outside the pears are starting to be ready to pick to ripen inside—pears ripen from the inside out on the tree so by the time they appear ripe they are often rotten! The pears are quite small this year. The June heatwave seems to have stunted their growth a bit. I will know to water them if that happens again next year. The mulled wine pear experiment from last Christmas may be duplicated en masse for presents this year.

The apples in the orchard are in wonderful form. I'm so looking forward to processing them in the dehydrator, as apple sauce, and of course just a whole bunch of gorgeous apple crisps because that is one of my favourite things of all time. Must remember to bulk order some cinnamon! My neighbour gave me an apple corer/peeler for my birthday! She laughed and said it was because she knows what my future holds! We might try some pressing too if we can borrow the equipment.

The flowers too are in full show mode and if the earth's joy was expressed as sweet peas and hydrangeas this might be heaven. The old lavender plants have bloomed so generously and the 50+ youngsters I've planted are even offering a small bloom or two. Happiness is seeing that. Truly.

About the Estate

The weather in August has been very interesting. It's been hot and sunny for a couple of weeks, but at the beginning of the month we had a storm where we had more rainfall in one day than most had ever seen. The water rushed off the hills behind us and the burns and channels about the houses almost didn't cope. Climate change is supposed to bring more of those types of events to this part of the world, so it was a good indication of some of the work that needs to be done. I've never seen it rain like that. Hardly any wind, just sheets of water for 24 hours straight.

All the creatures were hungry after hiding out for that one!

We've had 40 mph winds for the last 12 hours today. It's very strange to have this strength of wind on such a warm day. But it may have blown the midges that have been thriving in the warm, wet weather to some other continent! For some reason I was smart enough to check the weather so I was able to give my sweet peas some extra support and they made it through.

The pheasant chicks have gone down into the pens around the estate for the new shooting season so that curtails some of our adventures for awhile. But communication directly with the gamekeepers this year has really made the whole dog situation much more bearable. I am not required to have poor Alfred on a leash from the moment I leave my house. It all seems quite sensible this year. So I'm grateful for that. The men who are the gamekeepers are lovely people and that's part of the complexity of these sort of things.

There's a lot of trauma to the ecosystem introducing more than 1000 birds into this space every year and attempting to eliminate all the naturally occurring predators while they are at it. (It's not hunting I am opposed to, but this overly manufactured video game that is the shooting here that has no sensibility towards the environment or the sentient beings they waste). But what's exciting is this season really lights a fire under my desire to protect this space which means I've got to get to work on figuring out how to do it! Stay tuned.

Other Milestones

I'm so happy to report that these little letters have reached over 50 Patrons! How completely wonderful. Those of you who have been with me for a while will remember when we were trying so hard to get to 25. This means I'll also be pledging $50 USD per month to support organisations working on building connections, safe access, and diversity of community in nature and farming. I'm particularly interested in those working to build this for people of colour. Currently we continue to support Lemon Tree Trust (gardening support in refugee camps), Soul Fire Farm (ending racism and injustice in the food system in the US), Land in Our Names (working here in the UK to create more access to nature and farming for people of colour), Sundance Harvest in Canada, and I'll be looking for one to add in Australia this month.

Did you know in Scotland our Right to Roam laws mean everyone can go anywhere on foot? That means the country-side is actually available to explore. In reality there are so many more things that keep people from being able to enjoy it— transport, money, safety, skill sets and information on how to be there with intention and responsibility. But it's a start. Let me know if there are any local organisations doing work to make nature accessible that you are passionate about!

Lots of love,
Susie
xx

The role of the artist is to make the revolution irresistible.
- Toni Cade Bambara

SEPTEMBER 2020

The Gardeners Cottage
Argyll's Secret Coast
Scotland, UK

September 27, 2020

Hello out there!

Beautiful Yarrow above the loch. Yarrow is a healing plant, both for disturbed landscapes where it arrives first and for us.

I thought since I was so late and the way I was feeling in general that a grinning Alfred on the envelope was some of the medicine the world needed right now! The stamps are also a mish-mash as a new price increase on international stamps has occurred and I needed to use up some of the remainders from my stash. So hopefully Alfred distracted you from the lack of excitement there too.

I found it so hard to write this month. September was such a busy month with delightful harvests and need to process as much as possible of the bounty. I had a trip down south to clean out my flat which hopefully the sale will finish on shortly—if it feels like I've been talking about that for three months it's because I have! I have a hard time spending time indoors in this season when the weather is as good as it has been. Which makes me all sorts of behind on writing and painting and bookkeeping and housecleaning!

One of the things I love about writing to you is the way it helps me mark the passing of time and capturing the detail of seasons which pass so quickly. The details of the memories quickly blend away without such an effort. That's one of the great gifts of the world of plants and trees I feel. The way when they are thriving and allowed to do their thing they reliably remind us year after year of previous joys. For me it's one of the most important reasons to notice all the wonders from the dandelions' arrival to the caterpillars munching on the ragwort to the hawthorn blossoms transitioning into berries because in our world we are losing wild spaces so rapidly that even what we notice has diminished. It's called Shifting Baseline Syndrome. It means that even the level of wildness and the number of plants and creatures we expect gets smaller and smaller and each lower level normalised. And without the historical context we can't have an idea of what it was. Everything from the number of insects in the air at night that would have covered your windows as you drove down the road, to the sheer numbers of whales and fish that our healthy oceans supported. So if you're older take stock of what's missing in your world from your childhood.

Talk to young people about it. Figure out what of our everyday normal has taken it away and make small changes in your very own space. Miles of manicured lawns without dedicating space to the so-called weeds that are the food of the creatures that are missing? Chemicals...

One of the things that has been bothering me so much is how big a business it is to sell bird feed, but no one talks about how we need to keep spaces for bugs and caterpillars, and healthy soil filled with earthworms because birds don't feed their babies seeds. The little blue tit that I share so many pictures of, needs to feed about 700 caterpillars to its nest of young a day! It is a mark of our times to begin to reconsider what we do.

The threads of the web of life are so fragile at this moment. Most of the practices we have were created at times when it was considered an unbreakable chain of life. I honestly believe no one set out to break it, that was beyond the imagining of the people who were attempting to make life easier and more reliable for humans. But we know now that we can and did break it. And I believe that one of the places hope lies is through the hyper-local tending of the webs within our reach. What's in your reach? Where can you create a space for nature to do her thing without interference? It doesn't matter if it's only a window box. If you're lucky enough to have a garden can you rewild some of it and learn to take pleasure in the un-manicured thriving life that can arrive there. What of the more than human world is welcome in your reach?

In the Glasshouse and Gardens

Autumn is for Apples. So many wonderful, wonderful apples. All the neighbours on the estate spent three sunny afternoons clearing the or-

chard. The picking is the easy part, figuring out how to store them all away from the reach of the rodents is the big challenge! I bought a juice press and grinder and we pressed at least 12 L to see what we could learn. The juice was gorgeous. We have someone who is a brewer in our network who might advise about cider.

A very sad thing to report from the glasshouse. The grape crop was lost to an invasion of wasps and flies. I was in the glasshouse watering one morning when all of a sudden a buzzing descended. Every grape was covered and over a week they hollowed out most of the grapes leaving only the skins. It was both amazing to watch and very sad! Obviously I should have harvested earlier. But there are some very well fed pollinators in the world this autumn so I can't complain about that either.

But the tomatoes and cucumbers are still going strong. When I was growing up pickling and canning were always done en masse. Huge quantities collected and processed at once. My little garden produces differently of course and it's really a jar or two of pickles at a time as the ingredients are ready.

I've harvested the first sunflowers. I've got seeds drying in the kitchen for next year and some to eat. One head went to the birds out my window, two heads to the chickens. The goal this year is to make the five households on our estate and our immediate neighbour self sustaining for eggs. My contribution is to keep Alfred from torturing them—he likes to chase birds—and supply treats like sunflowers!

I've still got a fridge-full of pears to deal with and am determined to get some blackberries in the freezer too. But I'm trying to also prioritise other things that must be done and not worry that I'm "missing" everything! LOL My dehydrator has stopped heating all of a sudden and I've reached out for help from the Glasgow Repair Cafe. They are going to get me a video conference call with someone to help me diagnose and perhaps repair the problem myself! How wonderful. My first instinct still is to throw it out and get a new one. I really have to settle that part of myself down and say it's worth attempting to fix. My ripe pears are not worth another small appliance ending up in a landfill somewhere. If you don't know about Repair Cafe they are organisations all over the world that (pre-COVID) held monthly sessions where you could bring things in to get fixed. They usually have experts in many areas from sewing and patching, to electronics and mechanical things, etc. I have even had my knives sharpened in one. Check to see if there is one in your area and how they might be carrying on inside the current social distancing regulations.

Here is the glorious orange belly of the Great Crested Newt who is managing to grow in one corner of the walled garden despite Heron's best attempts to hunt it.

The More than Human World

It has become incredibly clear to me that my health and well being is tied to time spent in nature. Not necessarily doing anything in particular, just being with it, as it. It's not surprising to me at all that this month I had very little of the deep more than human connections that I have so come to rely on. The moments of noticed magic to report to you and hopefully inspire you to spot and share some of your own. In my (self) pressure to get the letter out and meet all my obligations this month I was trying to force my way through to production, at the cost of my well being. Again. Even for this beautiful work I cannot keep doing that. And I'm pretty sure you don't require that of me! And if I were to lose subscribers because a letter arrives late, that's so ok.

Change can only happen when we don't do new things the old way. Because the destination is eventually the one you were trying to avoid—in my case a deep habit of productivity and self abandonment in service of it and the external approvals that usually come with it. When I started to struggle at the emptiness of this section and the stress I was feeling, I remembered to set it down. I closed the computer and went for a walk. I sat on the hilltop table above the loch and a lone seal arrived and stared at me before getting on with her day. I watched her until the world came alive again and I could hear the little things, and see the clouds reflected in the still water protected from the wind by the little island. And I exhaled and found I indeed had things to tell you.

What makes a home?

I have been thinking a lot this month, with packing and cleaning out the flat and acknowledging the end of neighbourness, but not friendship, what makes a home? What makes me feel at home? I have had a lot of homes over the years. For the first time I realised how many goodbyes that includes as well as adventures. All the people I have waved goodbye to while I'm moving in what seems so unanchored a way to my next unfurling. Beautiful places and communities where I was happy and loved and thrived in at least a couple of ways. I easily sink into new community and I know that isn't true for everyone. I think gently of all the people who have never found home even right where they are from. I think of those who feel like they can't leave and pursue themselves to the next place that would provide a few new clues. I think of those who have to leave homes not by choice and what it takes to create another with that trauma. In my experience "home' is portable. And I just wonder if maybe feeling at home means knowing yourself in the present moment? Caring about your needs and dreams now, not stuck in the past or in the perpetual waiting game for the future.

When we trust that we are caring for ourselves we are able to begin to genuinely care for others, our communities, the planet. Not out of obligation (which ferments to a bitter taste), not out of an attempt to fill ourselves up (which drains and eventually drives away those we take from), but with generosity and the safety that only comes from being good with yourself. And no matter how much we might long for a particular place or viewpoint, being home in yourself is the truly priceless real estate.

Lots of love,
Susie
xx

You have been forced to enter empty time.
The desire that drove you has relinquished.
There is nothing else to do now but rest
And patiently learn to receive the self
You have forsaken for the race of days.
At first your thinking will darken
And sadness take over like listless weather.
The flow of unwept tears will frighten you.
You have traveled too fast over false ground;
Now your soul has come to take you back.
Take refuge in your senses, open up
To all the small miracles you rushed through.
Become inclined to watch the way of rain
When it falls slow and free.
Imitate the habit of twilight,
Taking time to open the well of colour
That fostered the brightness of day.
Draw alongside the silence of stone
Until its calmness can claim you.
Be excessively gentle with yourself.
Stay clear of those vexed in spirit.
Learn to linger around someone of ease
Who feels they have all the time in the world.
Gradually, you will return to yourself,
Having learned a new respect for your heart
And the joy that dwells far within slow time.

John O'Donohue,
"For One Who Is Exhausted, a Blessing."

OCTOBER 2020

The Gardeners Cottage
Argyll's Secret Coast
Scotland, UK

October 26, 2020

Autumn greetings dear
friends.

The clocks have changed
this weekend in Scotland and
it always discombobulates me
for a few moments. It makes
me feel like I'm behind in my

This was one of the most stunning
rainbows I have ever seen. We are in
the season of rainbows in Argyll now.
This is a scene across the Kyles of Bute
from Tighnabruaich.

day some how. Now that I try to pay attention to such things,
how amazing is the variety of triggers for self judgement! It
makes no sense, is completely invalid, and yet there I am doing
math in my head saying "well it's really 10am so you are behind
and are therefore horrible." I am so over entertaining that kind
of self talk. But that doesn't mean it doesn't come in uninvited.
These days I try to see it coming in and just open a door for it to
go right on by. Obviously it isn't as simple as that. For me it's
more like having a conversation with myself and then taking a
particular conscious action that demonstrates I don't agree.
Sometimes it looks like making myself another cup of coffee
and continuing to write this letter to you in my housecoat.

During an interview once the great poet Maya Angelou
talked about how she managed to prevent the seeping of small
ideas of unkindness or racism or sexism in her space. She
described a party at her home where she overheard someone in

a group indulging in some harmful conversation, like a racist uncle joke maybe, and from the other side of the room she simply declared: not in my house! And then showed them the door. And she was committed to doing that every time. She said it may exist in the world, but she didn't have to let it feed on her space. I always loved that. So when I have mean and unkind thoughts and catch myself I hear Maya Angelou in my head pointing the way out—not in my house.

My very first squash is still filling me with joy.

In the Glasshouse and Gardens

What is going on in my house however has gotten quite chilly! The weather has had a real change the last couple of weeks and I feel like it hasn't been a sunny day for a while. I'm exaggerating of course, but I wonder if the sensitivity to it is connected to the rising unease that has come with the second wave of COVID in our country and the stricter measures that entails.

I had such a lovely October planned! The most amazing visitors anticipated. People I have wanted to share this space with so much. The Scottish restrictions prevent people from visiting in each other's houses right now and all had to be cancelled. For the first time in all of this I felt quite isolated. I had a very random emotional/anxious wobble last week and of course it isn't random at all. So if you are feeling that way feel free to reach out at any time. We are all in this together for certain and I know for sure that we can still manage human connection from afar because we are doing that right here!

But the trees have been showing off anyway. I've collected acorns and chestnuts and have sown them in toilet paper rolls serving as planting pots in an attempt to help my neighbours have native trees from here to plant their new homestead (which I will lose them to in a couple of years).

As always in each of the seasons you can see the hand of the once head-gardeners in this place. There are bright red Japanese maples adding life and colour to the grounds and sweet autumn clematis climbing some of the walled garden. I had hoped to have firm, contracted, news to share with you about the garden, but we are still waiting for the paperwork that allows us as residents to take over the care of the walled garden! Keep your fingers crossed that there isn't anything ridiculous in the agreement and we can proceed. There are so many problems, but it would be completely lovely to be able to begin loving it where we can. So fingers crossed from next month I can be reporting to you about our plans and enacting them!

In the glasshouse the grapevine has mostly shed its leaves and I removed the fruit remains. It means there is more light, but feels very much like winter. I still have many things growing. The peppers that I nursed into growing at all have decided to flower at the end of October! Who know if it will be warm enough for them to actually fruit. I may move them onto my bedroom windowsill. I picked my first butternut squash and felt like a god. Winter kale and beets and cabbage are all in there doing their thing. I've planted a lot of garlic and onions outside for the first time ever. And I've managed to get my first 50 or so tulips and iris in a flower bed without anyone stealing them all yet. But it's very early days! Each day I watch the little native species red squirrel run by on its route—about 4pm every day like clockwork!—and I just sigh that it hasn't appeared to stop and take a tulip as it goes. I bought so many I have more to do, but am hoping to do some pots.

The More than Human World

October started off so perfectly with my first live visual of one of the otters that live along our coast. The shortening days mean their nocturnal habits come closer to my timelines. I had been at work in the gallery that day and when I took Alfred out on my return I had the idea that if I just went and sat quietly down by the boathouse I would see an otter. It was a beautiful evening and as I sat I kind of forgot about it. Then a flicker out of the corner of my eye and there

one was, swimming along the edge of the bay. I didn't get a
good picture, but it was such a thrill.

We are firmly into red deer hunting season here. The red
deer rut (breeding season) is one of the sounds in Scotland that
are still truly wild. As the stags come over the hills looking for
females and challenging intruders their calls echo off the stone
and carry across the water. Their roars penetrate walls and
drown out any other sounds when they are on the hills around
the cottage. The people making a life in this place have had
their survival linked to this species for ages beyond memory.
From a conservation point of view the fact that we have removed all predators of the deer from the ecosystem with the
exception of ourselves has led to an imbalance. There are so
many deer now and that is having a serious impact on the
health of the rest of the species of plants and animals and the
deer themselves. Basically on these islands, for those that eat
meat, we all need to eat more venison than any other kind.
Estates like ours are actually required by law to cull deer. And if
people aren't eating it, it goes to waste while industrial meat
production harms the planet. It just doesn't make sense. The
men that do the game keeping here—as an aside called Winston
Churchill Venison, I've met Winston and everything LOL—have
volunteered to do one of the deer for the residents. So I will be
expecting some hyper-local meat for the freezer soon. There
are also some amazing charcuterie businesses here in Scotland
that are making gorgeous venison products. I love and respect
the deer so much, daily I interact with their footprints and
droppings, walk down their trails, I thrill to see them, and I
don't want their deaths to be wasted. Once they would have fed
lynx and wolves and even bear as well as humans in this space.
We stacked that competition all in our own favour and then

decided that we preferred a neater source of meat. One where we didn't have to confront the creatures that come with it. And our dissociation with death has caused so much harm. I also completely honour and respect those who choose not to eat meat at all! It's complex and I think we are due as a species with working on the ability to handle complex truths and discussions. I know we are more than capable of it!

Samhain

I am writing to you just before the celebration of Samhain and Halloween and of course the letter will arrive to you awhile after. I am currently doing research for what I hope to be my fiction story inspired by this place, although I can tell you it surely doesn't feel like fiction to me as it visits and unravels inside my head. But I am researching St Ardmarnock —who there is really nothing about—by looking into the life of contemporaries such as St Columba of Iona. Scotland was a key location for the Christian conversion of these islands and as I read I'm struck with the idea that Rome might not have conquered this land above the Antonine Wall with soldiers, but there was a time when it managed it through the Catholic Church. I am currently lost in almost a century of debate about the disagreement of the correct dates of Easter and how those of Scotland and Ireland held out against Rome on agreement. And it makes me "smell something' that in the way of humanity it was probably about something much different than whether or not the 4th moon of the new year fell on a Sunday... which brings me back to topic that if any of the rituals for a change of season speak to you, just like Kat Golden of Gartur Stitch Farm says "the best loaf of bread is the one that you actually bake', the best marking of the seasons and our connection to the rest of the earth is the one that you do yourself.

The Celtic festival of Samhain is about the turning of the tides. The end and the beginning. It's a fire festival and has a lot of commonalities with the origins of Halloween and the Christian Day of the Dead. It seems all these blunt markers are a time for us to reflect on what we want to take forward into the winter—because remember things are happening in winter, deep below the surface—and what that will mean for spring. It's time to think of your ancestors and all that has brought you to this moment in time. I enjoy spending time thinking about this and will light a fire in my smoky hearth and do it this year.

May this letter find you safe and well. I'm sending extra love out to every one of you right now.

Lots of love,
Susie xx

So it's time for each one of us to evaluate how we can step forward now, and step up to the challenges of the times. Those of us who have been more comfortable, or who have felt safer, hiding in the shadows. Those of us who have hogged the light for all the wrong reasons. Those of us who have been lost and haven't known which way to go. All the exiles, the edge-dwellers, the non- belongers. The world needs us now; it's why we chose to be here. Haven't you always known it somehow, all along? Somewhere on the edge of a myth; somewhere in the deep forest of a story, somewhere in the drowning pool of a dream?
—**Sharon Blackie**, writing this month about the call of Samhain and these times.

NOVEMBER 2020

The Gardeners Cottage
Argyll's Secret Coast
Scotland, UK

28 November, 2020

My dear friend!

November has been a com-
plete rollercoaster to me. I feel
like the fact that I am upright
and full of joy today is a
miraculous occurrence, maybe
it always is though. The
month started with deep joy
as I got to welcome one of my

**The little Victorian dam and waterfall
on the estate, so very pretty and not a
great metaphor for forcing things!**

local-ish subscribers to the Cottage for a completely magical
visit (while following the COVID prevention rules). I'm so grateful for the two local friends and subscribers I have here in
Scotland because that is basically who has been able to come
visit since summer! Gail and Lynn you were boosts to my heart.
It's so fun though when people come who have been part of the
letters because I love to ask them what they want to see first?
Which tree or view or special spot to take it all in, because it's
familiar and unknown at the same time. Hopefully in the year
to come it will be possible for more of you to plan to come again
too.

Shortly after that lovely visit I got very ill. Not COVID thankfully, but my body was intent on releasing a lot. And that really
threw me for at least two weeks if I'm honest about it. I kept

thinking "Oh I feel like myself," but then I would be exhausted and unable to keep up with everything. The hubris in me that thought I was going as slow as I possibly could in this life right now! My body demanded slower and like any form of direction I fought it tooth and nail all month. I think I might learn the lesson in its entirety someday. Learn to never doubt my body when it asks for rest or quiet or solitude long before it shows me why it was asking.

And as I slowed down it also became so very clear to me that I am still decoupling/untangling excitement from production and trying to figure out how to take action without also forcing myself through things. Like the way water moves off the hills around me when left to itself. There are definitely some water-falls and rushing rivers that meet the sea, but most of the water doesn't progress in a straight line. There are lots of turns and pools to linger in and meeting up with others and allowing your shared momentum to carry you both further.

A beautiful shot of a sea eagle fishing from www.wild-scotland.org.uk

Stop the presses!

I had to come back to the letter and edit in a most remarkable occurrence! As I was on my very usual walk to the edge of the loch I could hear all the little birds and gulls making quite a racket. I didn't think much of it until I crested the last hill and I glimpsed the silhouette of a sea eagle sitting on the rocks of the little tidal island that is part of the bay at Black Harbour!!!

Those of you who have been with me for a while know how significant the eagle has been to me on this journey to move here and find my next steps in making a life. When I was trying to decide whether or not a move to Scotland was the right thing for me to do, I dreamed I was standing on one of Scotland's beautiful beaches facing the water and an eagle brought me a book. I basically found this house very shortly thereafter and stopped waiting for the perfect conditions and being attached to being able to buy what I thought I wanted. There have been so many more episodes with eagle and I keep learning more about this symbolism as I research the history of this area and try to discover the story I want to write about it. I was thinking in the new year I might keep myself more accountable and start sending you bits of the story each month too... but don't hold me to that just yet.

Anyway as I was struggling so much this month I asked for a little help in figuring things out and the next morning I was met by the great sea eagle calmly hanging out on the rocks near my favourite spot. The picture isn't very good as always I just had my iPhone with me. But it was a gorgeous morning and it let me come over two ridges until I was just across the tidal flood from it. Being watched and dismissed by an eagle is one of life's most wonderful things! The sea eagles (or white tailed eagles) are the largest bird of prey in the UK and the 4th largest eagle in the world. They were hunted to extinction here in the 1800s, but a successful reintroduction happened on the west coast in the 1970s and 1990s and this glorious creature near me is a testament to their success and the expanding of their territory south from the islands of Skye, Rum, and Mull. I had heard there were some at the north end of Loch Fyne and over near Loch Awe, but I hadn't seen any. And just like that a visit from one, just for me, just when I needed it.

Since I don't have a good shot of the eagle itself anyway, I thought I would show you how magical the morning was when it was here. Spot the eagle of the second rocks on the right hand side of the photo.

The Wild Things

With the exception of above, I have been mostly spending my time with trees and garden birds. The leaves have all blown from the oaks now too and the landscape is of their twisty wonderful shapes. It continues to astonish me how they bend and turn for balance against the harsh conditions—strong winds that can last a month, long periods of waterlogged ground that is not the most solid support, and such diminished daylight in the winter months. They are the hardiest of souls! I love getting up close and underneath them now while they invite much closer contact than when in their full impenetrable bloom.The mosses and ferns that they support even as they live and thrive are the brightest green and the softest sponge of a surface. I take a million photos a day, but will share a couple.

The feeding of the little birds are rapidly becoming one of my most regular outputs of income! As I write there are at least fifteen or twenty taking turns for a sunflower seed. All the excitement has brought a few extra species to check out what is going on. A stunning woodpecker popped by while I was on the phone the other day. And then a little falcon of some sort has swooped in a couple of times hunting for the little ones themselves. They all disappear into the hedge and holly, but not always fast enough. They like to come land on the window and look inside in case I am holding out on them I think.

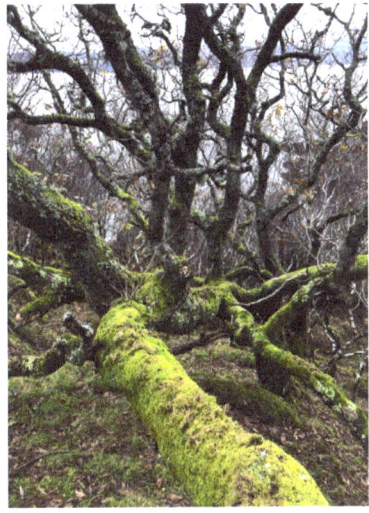

In the Glasshouse & Garden

In the glasshouse I'm pretty much wrapping up last year and starting on seedings for next. My experiment to get my tomatoes well into November didn't work very well, but I did manage to eat one fresh, ripened tomato right from the vine at the beginning of the month so I will call it a successful education. I'll have a bit better plan for next year and will get my second seeding done a bit earlier so the plants are more mature when the days start to draw in.

I am bound and determined to get my ranunculus to flower for me this year. They are the most beautiful flower. I realise that last year they were much too warm in the glasshouse once it got cooking and I will put them in pots this year for moving out. I've planted half of my bulbs now and will do the next half in January (I found a UK based tutorial for growing them online and am following her advice this year because I was rubbish!)

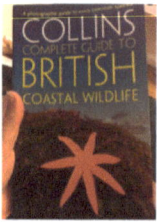

Top: My little bulb bed with a neat edge. Middle: My solar lights in the glasshouse which I love so much I am sharing again. Bottom: A wonderful gift this month. I will know everything shortly!

I still need to find time to move everything out and give it the big smoke out for pests. Every time the sun is out a couple of the flies that came with the great grape theft of September wake up and buzz around and remind me that they find it quite cozy and are willing to wait out winter with me. I keep chasing everyone out and opening the roof. This lets in my wrens and robins who are on duty for me. Inevitably once a week or so I lock one of them in overnight and they have a lot to say to me when I get up in the morning! Today the robin was waiting on the outside as soon as I turned on the kitchen light. Cheeky!

I also bought about 150 bulbs this year and have been slowly getting them into the ground or pots. I bought these very fancy tulips that I'm petrified to put out and lose to the creatures. I'm out of the wire I used in the one garden so now I'm trying to fool them with daffodils (which they won't eat) surrounding the tulips and dwarf iris. Spring will be very interesting! I managed to make my first edge around the pond outside the glasshouse doors. Just starting very slowly to reintroduce some edges and decoration while we slowly learn the rest. The garden isn't ours officially yet, but honestly I'm just going for it. No one is going to complain if it's more beautiful and I don't mind investing in the bulbs and maybe leaving them for others later.

Next stop Solstice

2020 has been such a strange year and yet for me it has flown by with a speed I've not yet experienced. If I think about it in a way I feel like it's still February! But this year wasn't having that. I so hope you and everyone you love are safe and well. The virus numbers here in the UK have led to a devastating death toll. I'm not sure when the shock wears off and the reckoning about what those daily numbers actually means happens. It's very very fortunate and yet completely weird to be untouched by it in actuality and yet also surrounded by it in reality.

But as always I take my solace from nature. And as the old woman roams the northern world as Winter right now, she will soon twist to begin the march south towards the middle to meet the maiden and turn the tide towards spring. Underneath it all the world is creating. Underneath all of this heaviness so are we. May whatever comes of us after these dark times be kinder and walk more lightly.

Until next month.

Much love,
Susie
xx

The Gardeners Cottage
Argyll's Secret Coast
Scotland, UK

December 2020
*(I've added to this letter on so
many different days and now I've
lost count!)*

**December I found myself chasing the
light around. It was painting something
differently each day and hour. From
the most dramatic silhouettes to
sunsets and rainbows, it has been the
loveliest month.**

Greetings dear friends and
warmest welcome to all the
new people who have joined
in this month.

It's such a joy to me to imagine these letters winging their
way from my little ideas and observations here in The Cottage
to your hands wherever you find yourself. This last year has
also taught us all not to rely on perfect timing as the efficacy of
the postal services around the world keeps flexing with the
pandemic response. So I decided that your December card
would be a bit more joyful and appropriate for whenever you
receive it! Like the daylight hours in December this last letter of
the year—old calendars and new—is shorter and hopefully
sweet and keeps us in the weight allowance for the letters!

December was a month full of lessons for me about bound-
aries and being true to myself in the face of different opinions
and social pressures. What a relief in life when you can finally
count on yourself to stick by you! I know that's a funny
sentence, but I think for those of us conditioned to please
people and make peace, the last person we tend to stand with is

ourselves if it causes any discomfort for others. I have often been guilty of the reasoning that "I can take it more easily" or "it costs me less" and so crossed some boundary or broke some agreement with my own beliefs. I got to practise not doing that a lot this month and though it was uncomfortable I can't believe how joyful it made me.

Winter primroses withstanding the frost.

In the Glasshouse and Gardens

As you can imagine it isn't really the season of growing, but more tidying and cleaning and the preparation work for the period from February on when we get to start seeding produce again in earnest. But there is some fun still going on. Can you believe I've spotted some daffodils already???

Some of my bulbs are starting to poke through the mulch as proof that we successfully managed to fool the creatures who prefer them as snacks to spring decoration! So far I have four of ten ranunculus popping up and this is 400% more than last year so I am thrilled. Gardening is such a humbling thing. The miracles are not much to your credit and your interference or mismanagement can be disastrous. But when the balance is found where you are supporting another living being correctly is one of the most beautiful things we can do to remember we are a part of nature too.

I've started on creating a stone and plant floor for the glasshouse. I'm collecting the stones almost one by one from the different beaches and bays around the estate. Carrying them back, laying them as level as possible, and then transplanting the springy, low Mother of Thousands.

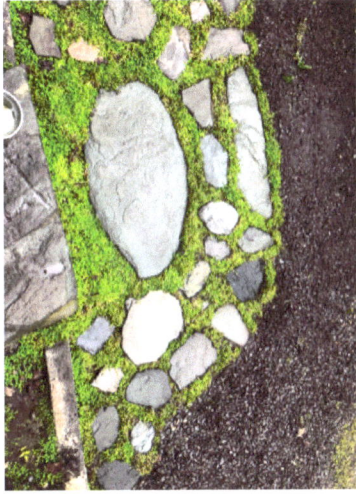

In December I found myself chasing the light around. It was painting something differently each day and hour. From dramatic silhouettes to sunsets and rainbows it has been the loveliest month. The little plant is already thriving in spots on the glasshouse floor and I've been thinking about how to incorporate it and yet not tear it up walking on it. It's a really resilient plant and can handle pressure, but I think the between stones part will really make it thrive. I'm using stones with so many of the characteristics that we find here. The sparkly one, the big pieces of shale, the seams of quartz. I've even got my neighbours in on it. I'm seriously in love with the idea and my goal is to get the first half finished by the end of the month.

We're still waiting for word about the walled garden and whether my neighbours and I will be able to be in charge of it. In the meantime I can't help myself and keep working on the edges. I've got the pond steps all cleaned out now and the tulips and iris planted (fingers crossed). I've decided that if I am going to ever achieve my dream of owning and caring for this whole place—still need to figure that out!—but that when that comes true I would regret the time that has passed while I lived here without offering the space some of the love I have. So four weeds pulled from the paths at a time as I walk to the compost bin, and sunny afternoons lingering and doing more. I am helping the space show itself well again.

The More than Human World

As fast as the lessons have been coming in December after the solstice, I'm also noticing nature coming so much closer. I'm not sure if this is because of hunger or the contraction of the days make us all active at the same time. But, each day right now it feels like the creatures have moved in, most welcome, a few degrees.

And not just my little Robin who I am slowly persuading to come to hand for food. We've just got to the point where it will come to my feet, but it is waiting for me many days when I return from the dog walk. It peeps to let me know it has arrived.

There are whole gangs of little birds that feed with me each day. Everyone seems quite hungry. I've even had a beautiful woodpecker come for the fatty worm cakes (the only feeder it fits on).

There was a doe casually walking down the road in front of the house with three pheasants following her. Herons and gulls are seeming to fly closer to my head on their way by. And the little red squirrels are coming to the yard and lingering. I bought myself a squirrel feeder, but don't have any evidence they've sussed it out yet. I don't know why, I'm just enjoying it all.

So I'll leave you this month with a little spell of magic from **JRR Tolkien** for the new year and a wish for all the hidden paths becoming visible to each of us.

> *Still round the corner there may wait*
> *A new road or a secret gate*
> *And though I oft have passed them by*
> *A day will come at last when I*
> *Shall take the hidden paths that run*
> *West of the Moon, East of the Sun.*

Happiest of New Years to you.

Much love,
Susie
xx

JANUARY 2021

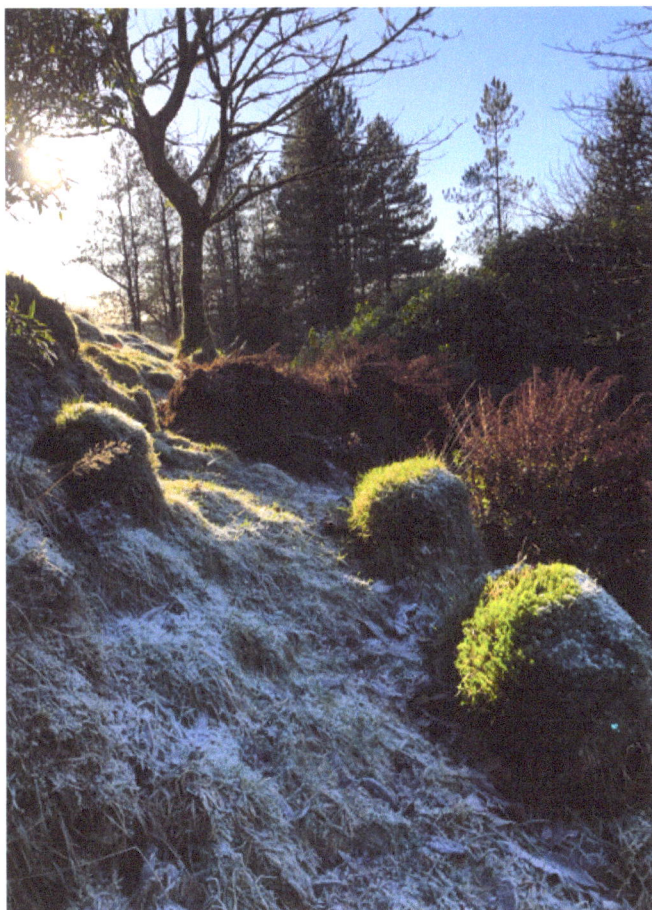

The Gardeners Cottage
Argyll's Secret Coast
Scotland, UK

28 January 2021

Dearest friend,

Warmest greetings from a damp and cold January day here in Scotland. We expect these things of January and frankly it has been so clear

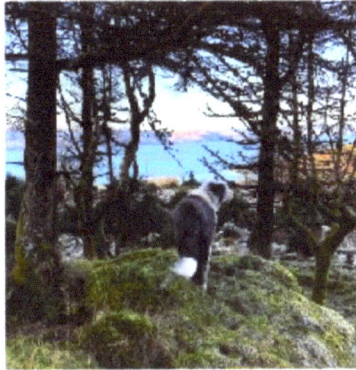

Alfred atop a lookout point amidst the Iron Age Fort on the estate that we spent time in this month.

and sunny for most of the month I have found it incredibly hard to be inside doing indoor tasks, so today it is welcome!

There has been so much to January already. I made a voice note on January 9th, to capture some of my thoughts to remember when I sat down to write to you, and I called it 'January Part 7000." Which made me laugh today. It's really quite amazing how much we are capable of learning and recalibrating to even when it doesn't feel like that is what we are doing at all!

In one of my notes I was thinking about my creative process these days and how I can't force it in any way. I can't tell myself when I will have it and I certainly can't tell myself what form it will take. I can sit in the most pleasing spot with the most beautiful journal and pen in hand ready to capture the experience of this time and space and be able to transcribe none of it into words. I get pulled to painting the kitchen cupboards instead. Or setting stones in the floor and weeding pathways.

I haven't been still for much of January and a part of me longed to be at my desk, to begin writing the stories that are living in me but don't want to be born yet. And surely deep winter is the time for that! So I get angry at myself for not being creative "in the right way!" My productive mind is yelling "you are procrastinating!" But time after time I learn this lesson to follow my body a bit more. The repetitive thought-free making of things relaxes and nourishes me in a way that the creative crucible never does.

My maternal grandfather Gabriel was a gardener and a maker of practical things out of wood. When he retired he was always in his garden and taught so many of us the (words he would never have used) grounding and meditation of hands in the dirt. He was also a father of eight who lost most of his stomach to ulcers from worrying. I wonder today how much he worried about all of us even later in his life... I think he found his own way to drop those thoughts and burdens, at least for a time, through a relationship with the slower deeper hum of working in the soil.

And as I begin to rebuild my own relationship with creativity and how I want to be in the world it made me think about all the "beautiful" things I thought I had done, some of which I forced myself to do in a particular way or time. And how they couldn't have been entirely beautiful because they had come out of a place of force. So I'm curious to what I might be able to create now without it.

A Visit to Ancient Times

On a sunny but frozen day in early January I packed myself a thermos of tea and headed up to the Iron Age Fort site that sits atop a hill on your way down the long estate road. Visiting the ancient world is only a short walk away I can see the tree covered shape of the hillside from many windows in the cottage.

The little sign indicating the path up to it is one of the first things you see as you turn parallel to the loch and start making your way down towards the cottage. And in the way many things are at Ardmarnoch, the sign points to an almost indiscernible path leading into thick rhododendrons surrounded by deep mud that you can't image you'll quite make it through! I had never been to the top before and the fort had been calling me for a little while. I knew the frozen ground made the perfect day. So my faithful companion and I set off.

The Iron Age in Scotland is mainly considered the time between 700 BC and 500 AD. Basically the period which is the end

of "Ancient History" in Europe. There aren't walls or things left up there. It's mostly carved levels and circling pathways which once would have allowed more and larger traffic to make its way up. The views are sweeping and of course a brilliant defensive spot. The light was spectacular. I spent hours up there. I explored and looked for the cup-marked rocks unsuccessfully. But mostly I was taken over with a sense of wonder of connections through time.

I sat on a lovely tree trunk that seemed to grow in anticipation of my visit and drank my tea and thought about the community that would have been here. A people untouched by the Romans and before the Vikings came for the gold in the monasteries and only seeing the beginning of the ancient kingdom of Dalriada. All the feet that covered this ground. How something that feels so untended would have been busy and important. I thought about who they were defending themselves from and why. When I made my descent back into the real world of here and now I felt like I had gone somewhere completely different for awhile.

Dalriada, Irish **Dál Riada** or **Riata**, Gaelic kingdom that, at least from the 5th century AD, extended on both sides of the North Channel and composed the northern part of the present County Antrim, Northern Ireland, and part of the Inner Hebrides and Argyll, in Scotland. In earlier times, Argyll had received extensive immigration from the Irish (known as Scoti until the 12th century) of northern Ireland and had become an Irish (i.e., "Scottish") area. In c. 500, the ruling family of Irish Dalriada crossed into Scottish Dalriada and made Dunadd and Dunolly its chief strongholds. Irish Dalriada gradually declined; and after the Viking invasions early in the 9th century, it lost all political identity. Heavy onslaughts from the Picts checked the Dalriada of the Scottish mainland. In the mid-9th century its king Kenneth I MacAlpin brought the Picts and Scoti permanently together, and thereafter the whole country was known as Scotland.

The More than Human World

As you know if you've been with me a while one of my chief delights is the amount of bird species that surround the cottage. Your envelope this month features the Great Spotted Woodpecker. I have a female that visits the bird

Daily robin time is good for my soul.

feeder outside my desk window most days (she likes the fat squares and hammers away into them). It brings me such pleasure to see her. That shock of orange-red on her belly and the bright and crisp black and white pattern is so startling. The one I painted for you is a male though as they have the extra spot of orange on the head and I can't always be trusted to paint the whole bird in the space allowed!

I have been finding myself seeking the companionship of the natural world far more than humans at the moment. I don't know if that's because it's important that we all begin to re-make space for that relationship if we are going to undue the harm we have done... but it's a call I can't ignore and seem to feel most at peace in it. I have multiple little robins who will take food from my hand now! They follow me about the yard and I know the sound they make when they've spotted me.

The one I started with in the front of the house is pictured here. I feed it everyday on my return from walking the dog. It has started to sing to me on some days before it feeds and my heart almost bursts out of my chest. And then somehow I've ended up with two more in the walled garden! These two are funny and the one who I gather is not supposed to be in that particular spot (when the other one shows up it always chases it away) is the braver and even has no qualms with hopping about Alfred's feet. I feed this one on the low edging wall just past the greenhouse. And somedays once it has taken the food from my hand I simply empty my handful of food on the rock beside me and sit in companionship with it while it eats. One morning it finished and just hung out in companionship with me. I don't have words to describe that feeling.

We had a very dramatic incident this month as a whale skull and some other bones washed up on one of our beaches. After my neighbours discovered it I headed out with a tape measure and camera so I could report it to the Scottish Marine Animal Stranding Scheme. Since 1992 this organisation collates all the data of strandings or dead cetaceans (whales, dolphins, porpoises), seals, basking sharks or marine turtles around Scotland with the purpose of gathering scientific data about the health and ecology of these species as well as information for conservation and measuring human impact. They share their data on the internet for everyone to access.

I really wanted to do the report, but it took me a week or so to go to the find because honestly the idea of facing the dead whale felt like a lot to me. I have loved whales and dolphins my whole life. Every trip I take to different parts of the world I have always tried to incorporate some time seeking them out. The humpbacks singing in northern British Columbia and playing in Baja, Mexico. Orcas in the Pacific Northwest. The great Blue Whales in the Indian Ocean surfacing between massive tankers and looking unimpressed and exhausted with us following. I love knowing these creatures are just out in the open water around me here. I love seeing porpoise from the ferry deck as I run an errand. I hate that we are losing them through what we've done in this world. So for me they weren't just bones to count and physically spending time with the proof of their loss was hard for me.

When I arrived at the beach it was even more difficult as the sea had decided to place the skull next to the new carcass of a grey seal. It was like I was not allowed to retreat into scientific endeavour with fascinating, fleshless bones. Nature was making me

The whale skull as I found it on the beach. You can see the distinct shape of the skull and the breathing hole clearly.

face it straight on decomposing flesh, overwhelming smell and all. I stood there for a moment and decided my prayer for them was that I wouldn't let their deaths go unremarked and I got to work.

When I reported the skull it was identified as a Northern Bottlenose Whale and told it was quite a find! These lovely creatures are described as friendly and inquisitive with gentle dispositions that had been mercilessly exploited by humans because of it. It's estimated that 65,000 were taken in the 19th and 20th Centuries. They are still killed in the Faroe Islands today. And noise pollution and plastic are other threats. We don't have enough data about them to even give them a proper conservation status.

The males grow to be over 11m long and weigh 7500 kg. They are recognised by their large foreheads. They eat deep-water squid, herring, prawns, sea cucumbers and even starfish.

As I thought about writing this story to you this month I had this awful thought that when I'm in my 90s people would come and talk to me because I had seen so many whales and we just don't have them any more. I'm not interested in that being something that comes true. All is not yet lost. And I feel in the depth of my bones that us beginning to notice things around us, both their presence and their absence, is one of the most important things we can do to begin to mediate the impact our individual and collective lives have on the non-human things that we share this planet with.

Much love,

Susie

xx

Attention is the beginning of devotion.
- Mary Oliver

FEBRUARY 2021

The Gardeners Cottage
Argyll's Secret Coast
Scotland, UK

February 23, 2021

Greetings from wet and
windy Scotland on this day.

I'm pretty sure I found a portal to somewhere here! As usual I sent Alfred through to test. He didn't come back with any interesting tales.

February is one of my favourite months! No really. Even when the wind is blowing a gale or a hoolie (such a great word) at 50 mph and the rain can move through the sky like a wave too. Even then. Here at the Cottage there are so many reasons why February is a favourite. February 1st is the last day they can shoot pheasants. So once that passes there is no "out of bounds" any more for the dog and I on the estate. From August to February the prevalence of the pheasant and partridge pens take up some of the very best walking spots on the estate. And because I'm a good tenant and not because it's the law, I don't go near them (mostly). So in February Alfred and I head out further in and farther up as CS Lewis wrote and it's wonderful.

In February the bracken is well and truly dead and broken down. This means all the wonderful deer trails and hidden rock formations or mysterious stone placements show themselves. It's like maximum viewing time of the bones of the landscape here. It informs my lush summer wanderings and what paths to try and keep clear. And in February there aren't any ticks yet!

So the dog isn't medicated and I don't have to check myself for hitchhikers if I've been a little too far off the path and pushed my way through bushes.

February is when you really feel the return of the light and we cross the 10hrs of daylight mark. They say that's when everyone starts to grow and you can feel it. It also helps you treasure the accessible starry sky (not having to stay up really late to see it like summer). The last trip outside with the dog is usually star-drenched or drenching, not much in between! One of my favourite things is walking past a window in a darkened part of the house and twinkling stars catching my eye. The windows become picture frames of the cosmos. It's something that just doesn't happen when you live in a town filled with street-lighting. So I love that too.

I'm in pretty good form then it would seem this month! Thank goodness for that.

Higher, higher and always a hundred stops for the view.

About the Estate

We've had all the weather this month. It went from frosty and even a bit of snow on the ground to wildly windy and heavy downpours. And then there have been these gloriously sunny days where inside work feels impossible and I fall behind completely.

I thought I would share lots of photos from our walks into the areas I haven't been for a while. There are so many wonderful ancient oaks and little pathways. I found a particular part of the stream that just yelled for the neighbour children to be splashing and playing in it and so we all went there one day for a picnic.

The snowdrops are in bloom and the daffodils are beginning to tease. One or two in really sheltered spots have opened, but most are a bit more sensible and are just fortifying the stems and leaves until this month goes by I think.

After last month's dramatic skeleton finds it has been quite quiet on the discovery front. Although another neighbour last autumn had found a dead bird at the beach who had a leg ring. He removed the ring and put it in his pocket because as he said "I could hear you in my head telling me that we would need to report it." I love being that voice of our little community! But he lost the ring somewhere on his way home. Never mind, months later it was found by the swings of all places. I quickly reported and it was found to be a young Shag who had been tagged as a nestling about 20 kms north of here near the top of the loch. It never made it passed its first year.

162. CORMORANT, *Phalacrocorax carbo*

163. SHAG, *Phalacrocorax aristotelis*

The illustration to the left shows you what a Shag looks like. They are quite large birds and you can tell by the leg tag in my hand. They are very similar to the Cormorant and we have both along the coast here. I love that by simply filling in forms and taking pictures we are contributing to caring for the animals around us in this very special place. Also I know my subscribers outside the UK will be wondering what is it with British birds' names being interchangeable with cheeky things?! It took me a long time to be able to talk straight-faced about all these Shags and Tits. It's good for extra humour I think.

The birds continue to be a treasured feature this month. As I was uncovering some of the plants this morning in the glasshouse I realised that atop a number of fence posts in the walled garden Song Thrushes had arrived this morning. The world was alight with their beautiful song and I just stood there with my coffee in my housecoat and slippers and listened to their symphony. All the little birds are making so much more noise. Not just my beloved robins looking for food. It makes you turn off the radio so that the house is penetrated with the sound. No need of a chime or a gong to clear energy here!

As for the little robins they are well and I have a couple of them now flying to my hand to take their mealworms. One has landed, but mostly it's still a hover operation. I love them. Which is obvious because I never stop talking about them.

Another ancient oak mapped. This one looks like it fell over a hundred years ago and kept going. Talk about trees that try!

In the Glasshouse and Gardens

Oh my goodness I have been having fun in the glasshouse! And outside too actually. I've managed to get the big bed outside the guest room nicely cleared and mulched. It's ready for its second year lavender hedge this summer and the tulips and daffodils I planted last fall are starting to poke out. Is there any more joyous feeling than a bulb poking its head through the soil?? I'm not sure how many I've gotten past the creatures— but hopefully enough to have something beautiful to show you next month.

I've started many veg and more flower seeds. I might need to admit I'm always way more enthusiastic about flowers until it's almost too late and I really want to be growing food! I'm trying to balance that better. My wonderful neighbour at Crispie Estate has gifted me a whole bunch of large used garden pots and I cannot wait to have them filled will ranunculus in a couple of months. Then they will go on duty with the climbing sort of veg, but first total flower decadence! I'm trying to have a better plan for the growing space in the glasshouse all while retaining the beauty of lushness of a space you want to spend time in. At the moment it's a bit of a mess. The floor isn't quite done and all the apparatus of summer, pots and canes and compost, are piled and waiting to be deployed. But each day gets a little neater and things get clearer.

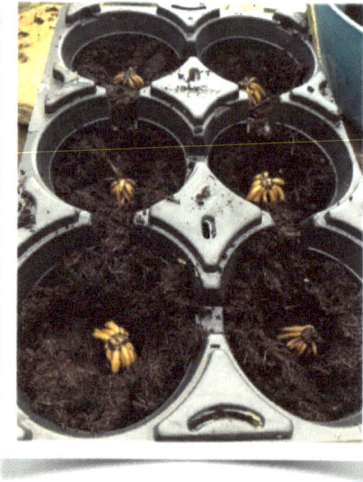

More ranunculus corms going in. I may have a problem. Send help (or vases).

We still haven't had word about our approval for the walled garden—despite many asks. I continue to quietly work on parts that are heritage flower beds so as not to lose what is there. I've pruned roses and also ordered 100 gladioli bulbs in some "just pay shipping" promo. I'm such an easy mark! But I will put them in one of the protected beds under the pear trees and see if it won't be a complete delight this summer.

It's one of the things I love about life here that I didn't have before. I'm getting so good at planning and commitments! I used to always think—I have no idea where I'll be or what I'll be doing in four months! So I didn't sow the seeds of future pleasures and accomplishments. Looking back I think that was one of the causes of my restlessness and searching. It feels very different right now. In both work and gardening I am addicted to sowing the seeds and watching them become something delightful and nourishing.

From the House

I finished my kitchen cupboard painting and am still in love with the results. I've also decided that one of the things that has become completely necessary is having help cleaning the house. I am just not any good at prioritising that job! Having regular guests was fabulous for keeping me on pace, but since the pandemic it's truly the last thing I do or want to do! I'm tidy, but I hate cleaning and its un-doneness weighed on me. So when my neighbour was commissioning a service to come out this way and I could hop on for an hour a week (which no one would come this far out for exclusively) I did. I thought it might be time for me to prioritise the things that care for me too. Even if it feels decadent. After all this time I'm still not that good at that. I've already noticed a difference after a couple of weeks and I'm so grateful for disposing of another "should" about life. (And it's all done very COVID sensitive incase you worried.)

And I'm so happy to report that the softcover edition of Letters From The Gardeners Cottage, the collection of the first year of letters, is finally here! Those of you who did the promotion will have yours enclosed with this letter. I'm working on the plans for its wider release into the world. I've been feeling a little tender about it. Shy almost. Those feelings confirm for me how important this work is to me. How blessed I feel to be having this experience and sharing it with you.

Your support is what has made this possible. You've done that both financially and for the fact that you are interested at all! Every month my courage grows and I feel more prepared and solid about sharing this experience and story with others. I thank you from the bottom of my heart and I am certain something good is being woven amongst us all and here at The Gardeners Cottage itself.

Much love,

Susie

xx

If you've never experienced the joy of accomplishing more than you can imagine, plant a garden.
- Robert Brault

MARCH 2021

The Gardeners Cottage
Argyll's Secret Coast
Scotland, UK

March 28, 2021

Dear friends,

I find this process of
monthly letter writing quite
an eye-opener about how
much happens in the months
of our lives. Historically I

My robin friend who now flies into my
hand and hangs around a bit before
leaving. It's wonderful.

would have hurried passed while new things and attention-
needs arose. Always intending to remember what happened,
but inevitably losing most of it. The amazing part of this
process is the dwelling in the moment just a little bit longer.
Sticking with it just long enough to document or explain or just
share with you. And I'm grateful for that treasure.

March was one of those months that stated slow and picked
up pace and if it wasn't for my notes I would forget that. Early
in the month I wrote a line of remembering for how I was
feeling.

You can't command the sap rise.

Walking under the trees that had not yet begun to bud while
so many other spring enthusiasts were flashing and popping all
around them made me understand my own body a bit more,
again. By commencing this new life that has at it's foundations

a desire to untangle from an oath to over-productivity and over-work, I inevitably hit a wall where my body and my mind have two different ideas. My mind knows what to do next and what actions are needed and it also screams "NOW" a lot. My body says: not yet. There is a cost to birthing ideas and holding space and doing work and making change. It needs me to add rest and observation to my skill set. In the old days before I gave my body any voice or vote besides illness, I would have just pushed on and through. I did that for decades and the result is now I literally can't. The full stop comes on much faster. So finding ways to be a contributor without the futile attempt to force the sap in myself to rise on command is part of the journey I am on. It causes me anguish sometimes. But in the end when I follow my internal tides I find I not only get further, I manage to do it without hurting myself. Entering into a deepening relationship of trust in myself and my timing is extraordinary. And when it is hard and I don't know what to do with myself I go feed a robin.

The weather has been as changeable as my energy sources, but definitely loving the extended sunny days. It makes the entire world feel lighter and fulfils the most ancient promise that life returns.

In the Glasshouse and Gardens

I have the best possible news! It's finally happened. We, the residents of the estate collectively, have consent to take over the walled garden and care for it. After two years of rational contract attempts, the current owner of the estate said "can't we just do it without a contract?" Seriously.

The contract though was for our protection as the owner is quite impulsive and we didn't want to make any great investments and not be protected from him deciding something outlandish. So as a group we have decided to just begin to love it and do some work to help what's there have a chance to be its best for now. It's a complete mess. The drainage is still messed up and it won't allow wide-spread cultivation without addressing that. But already there are little flowers that never showed themselves before all

The before (current ownership) and after in the walled garden.

of a sudden popping up to show us where they are, where the rushes need to be cleared first, etc.

I also learned that when the estate was purchased the only thought the owner really gave to the garden was considering it for a dog run. That explains everything about the way it has been treated. It was once a rich and fertile source of food and flowers and beauty. One of the difficulties, because we care about such things, is that through the neglect the wilded parts of the garden have also become a habitat for lovely things like the newts, slow worms, and toads etc. So we are not just randomly cutting everything that we won't be able to keep up or aren't intending to replace. It will be a more patient restoration. If you look at the picture I've included you can see what it looked like a decade ago. Already on its way into decline.

So we are leaving the grass bits rushed at the moment—there is no need for more lawn. We are tackling the paths with each household adopting a part. I am leading the restoration of the flower beds along the wall by the greenhouse and the recutting of the access paths in the closest square so we can familiarise ourselves with the flowers that remain there. From the last two years I know it's quite a few. There are many isolated treasures to shower with love and attention. I've pruned rose bushes and clematis and spotted the perfect place for 100 gladioli bulbs.

So exciting!!! My reward for finishing my computer work is to get to go garden. I can't wait to keep you up on the progress.

In the glasshouse so many wonderful things are happening. The apricot and peach are in full blossom and the warm weather spells saw the bees emerge to help with pollination! Yay! I got to retire my feather for pollination assistance this year.

The seeds are germinating quickly and strongly. I worry that I've planted more than I can manage inside again! Although we can do some experimentation outside this year. So exciting!!! I'm committed to attempting to grow as many sunflowers as I can in one of the sunny protected corners of the garden. If it works it will be glorious and lots more food for all of our little birds.

The floor of the glasshouse was also the toad romance centre of the estate this month. Thankfully it seems to be over. But I was planting and potting to the calls of the males to the females. I don't know too much about the process, but mostly the males grip on to the female's back for dear life and hold on until she's ready. They then fight each other for that spot with some nasty back leg and claws action. I found them stacked three high at one point and another with a big gash out of his neck. Hopefully they can all be resting now knowing the next generation is safely on its way!

Around the Estate

One of the ways I am starting to reclaim and document the natural world that is found so abundantly here on the estate is through participating in the citizen recording projects. Just like we reported the whale skull and the shag leg tag, there are more organisations that track species living presence and diversity around the UK. I participate on one called iSpot. ispotnature.org There are also lots of wonderful experts on there that can help with species ID confirmation. I'm really enjoying using it and want to remember to do it more—even with more common species, because let's be honest we can't guarantee that will stay true and we have so gradually lost many of the species that we assumed were doing fine until it was too late. By cataloguing the wonderful sightings and encounters that I have I am contributing over time to the argument for why this landscape needs to be protected. I feel good about that.

One of the exciting episodes this month came when they neighbours caught sight of one of our resident Tawny Owls in the daylight. The soundscape of the evenings here are often filled with the sounds of the owls. It's wonderful, but we don't often get a glimpse. I've included a wonderful picture of it asleep in the tree by the road. Tawny Owls are large and very capable predators. It was exciting to get to see one so clearly.

Ulli Mattson photo.

I also had a wonderful walking adventure up to the top, east boundary of the estate. Up between the high hills of Craig Mhor and Beinn Sheiag. I found the beautiful remains of one of the estate walls. Pressed up agains a commercial forestry crop on the other side, and a beautiful old Larch tree coming into bloom. The wall was covered in moss and was high and sturdy and you are instantly transported back in time when you encounter these forgotten (for the moment) masterpieces. It was an incredibly special spot and definitely on the picnic destinations for the more robust visitors.

The daffodils and primrose are ruling the land though and oh my is it a pleasant thing. I've told you before that there are thousands of them. And taking their picture is something I do on a daily occurrence trying to find an angle that shares with you how completely wonderful it is to have your head turned over and over to this joy.

My reward for finishing your letters will be to go out and collect one of all the types that I can find! Last year I managed six. I think I've spotted more this year! It's amazing how your eye gets better informed all the time.

Much love,

Susie

XX

The high boundary wall and the lovely old larch.

It is spring again. The earth is like a child that knows poems by heart.
- Rainer Maria Rilke

APRIL 2021

The Gardeners Cottage
Argyll's Secret Coast
Scotland, UK

April 28, 2021

Dear ones,

I'm writing you on the
second anniversary of my
move to the Gardeners Cottage. Two years drenched in

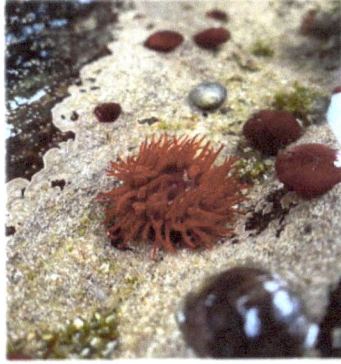

Lots of time this month spent gazing
into tide pools and filming anemones.

this light and often rain. Two years of the contrast of explora-
tion and hardly leaving home. A year of welcoming others and a
year of solitude.

There are so many things that are part of me now that
weren't before.

I know hundreds of new names of plants and animals—even
rocks!—which surround me that I hadn't met or noticed before
I came here.

I've learned to be brave and get introduced to so many wild
plants for eating that I'd never tasted or gathered.

I know now that I love the scent of nettle as it's getting
picked. Something pings viscerally in me when I smell it. The
relief of hungry, vitamin-depleted ancestral genes celebrating
its spring arrival. It's like they can't help but celebrate in my

Counting daffodil species.

body that centuries-felt sign we've survived another winter and help has arrived.

I can pick and clean mussels for dinner. I know where each kind of seaweed grows and which ones taste like truffles and which ones to put on the garden to fertilise it.

I have learned to grow some of my own food in the most pleasing way.

And I've learned how to tease sweet peas up the side of a house. And found so much joy in the actions of seeding and watering and potting and picking.

I've learned that all things do not have the quick pace of somethings and they are worth the wait. If you can't wait, don't bother because you can't force them to be ready until they are.

I've taken joy in preserving the bounty of this landscape. Each year the offering slightly different in flavour and scale. Jams, chutneys, pickles, booze... all a complete joy to make and share. There is nothing so satisfying as pulling out your dried cherries and currants from a summer almost as far away as one can get to flavour your own hot cross buns in spring.

I found the pace of a day that brings me ease and peace.

I learned to like the look of my face without any prep work.

I know the feeling of the water of the loch on my skin every month of the year.

I've come to an amazing relationship with my body these days.

Fluffy baby robin.

My fat, 49 year old body with its crooked feet and knees that cause all sorts of trouble. It has been amazing to me. And I actually have a relationship with it now in a way I never did before. I'm not sure I could have ever come to that in the presence of others. There are just too many layers of society that police women's bodies so relentlessly that even people who love us aren't always safe to be near. I'm not sure I was capable of it and I know from experience I'm still not always capable of

Uncovering old choreography in the walled garden.

it now. But when we are alone, my body and me, I can be trusted not to be ripping myself apart.

I've learned so much about self worth and money.

I've learned the names of new stars, what it feels like to walk in the night by their light only.

I've learned to tell the difference between owl species and even the gender of the Tawny Owls that chorus around the cottage each night. I'm so grateful for friends who have helped tune my ears to birdsong.

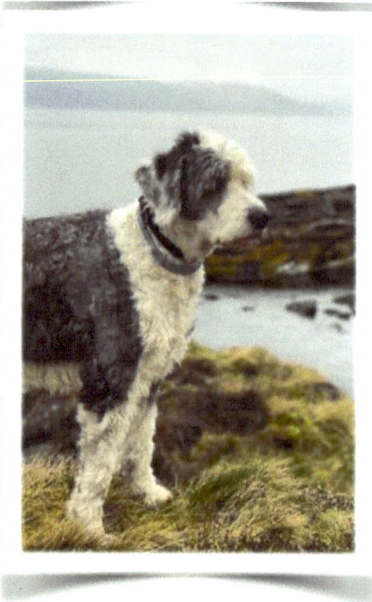

Alfred turned 6 this month. He's as photogenic as always.

I've learned how much the little birds bring me joy and how much we've become part of each other's universe this year.

I've learned the sound of the wind arriving and how it sounds different in the Cedar than the Birch or Beech.

I've learned to love the tricky Larch with it's shedding needles, perfect pinecones and pink blooms.

I remembered the part of me that always, deeply, claimed her spot as part of nature. I can't believe I got away with denying her this honestly. Maybe I didn't.

I have walked down paths that the deer have kept open for longer than anyone knows. I have heard the Red Deer stags roar in rut and know the warning bark of a Roe deer when they've spotted the dog.

I've learned how deep my grief is for this planet we are losing. When I step on a beautiful piece of moss on the seashore and hear the plastic in the ground underneath me crack... When the whales swim in to die... when no one is counting or noticing the bugs that are gone and when everyone is still using pesticides and herbicides and cutting down trees for some wholly human-created aesthetic... when everyone who has a child is not fighting harder to protect their likelihood of thriving into the future... I have spent a great deal of time in heartbreak here.

I've also learned that its very hard for me to be here and not be able to care for this land. I'm learning to be with it and yet not necessarily be able to do much for it beyond witness it. Maybe that's all it's asking of me.

And I've learned that your support of me here in this way is one of the most surprising and delightful endeavours I've yet met in all the things I've ever done. I mean that truly. That it brings you pleasure to receive these missives is my joy. That you've written back to me over the years, beautiful things, has always been a surprise and delight. That we've built this little web of love and understanding around the world—that the nature I observe here brings me joy, then travels through a letter and brings you joy, well surely that has to be its own kind of magic. So thank you.

In the Glasshouse and Gardens

I think most of you (in the northern hemisphere) have had a similar April—winter, drought, heatwave, and spring all trying to happen at once. It's been intense for the little things.

Indoor tulips giving be joy.

Lucky for me the glasshouse is generous with its climate and the only problems encountered are operator error on pots being left outside or out of the propagator. But things are going really well. Many things are up and even in their summer grown spot. Other trays of seedlings are being patient with me and the weather.

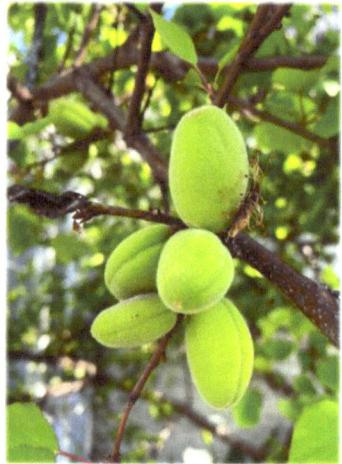

Apricots! Thank everything.

In the Walled Garden I have been so busy! The beds leading away from the glasshouse along the wall have been half reclaimed. I know what mostly grows there so it was easy to clear and prep. Still it has managed surprises of neglected treasures who have found a way through.

I've started the attempt at cutting some paths through the big, wild flower square that would once have had a lovely little internal walk through. There is so much to do out there and at first I got a little lost in trying to do it all. Then I remembered a couple more things: it is not my garden; my pace is perfect; any love is more than its had in a very long time, what I have to give —while still earning a living and not breaking my body—is enough.

Around the Estate

If you follow my posts on Instagram you will have seen that the robin parents had fledged the first batch and brought me this youngster to be fed. It was one of the most touching things ever, that these little, fragile, sovereign creatures found me safe enough to bring their children to visit. Oh my. The father robins are the ones who care for the fledglings while the mother prepares for the next set of eggs. Robins can do three batches a year!! Robin- daddy as I call him has been completely wonderful and having the proximity to watch him care for the baby has been a joy. A couple of weeks into life outside the nest the baby arrived with a horrific injury to its eye and I couldn't tell if it had lost it completely. I prepared myself to its loss, but was so hopeful when everyday it was there for some meal worms and its dad was feeding it and responding to all its peeps. I'm very happy to report that the injury healed and the eye is still there! So my first baby robin has at least as good a shot as any of making a life of its own.

Animals were really the focus of the month because I had the most gorgeous otter sighting as well. Alfred and I had walked to the Secret Beach.

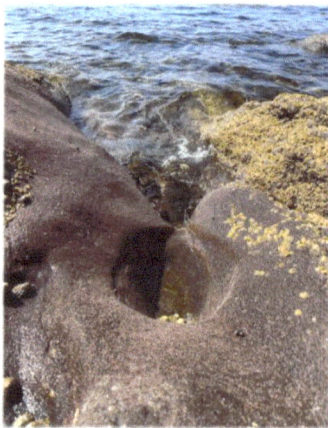

The goddess rock.

I've hurt my knee again and we were staying pretty close to home, but one morning I felt like I was supposed to go and visit what I call the Goddess depression in the shore rocks next to the Secret Beach. It's about a mile or so away and I was just determined to go very slow. When I got there it was as wonderful as always and I was taking some pictures of the Goddess after we'd had our talk and just found myself sat on the rocks for about half an hour. Alfred was close to me just chilling too.

All of a sudden in the water I saw what at first looked like sea weed floating, but it was moving too deliberately and it was a very strange shape! In retrospect an otter carrying a very big crab, claws pointed to the sky from each side of its head, can look a great deal like a mythical creature! But I quickly realised what was happening and started to film it. It turned out to be a young otter and it was such a treat to watch it come out of the water with its lunch and climb up the rock face to find a spot with a view to enjoy it.

This morning as I left the house for a walk with Alfred, just a little bit earlier than usual, I looked across the field that falls to the north of The Cottage and a herd of about 7 red deer were making their way across. They were about half a mile away, but crispy clear with their dark coats against the still deadened grasses. It made me remember how truly enormous they are. The delicate little Roe deer that come closer to the houses with their tiny little hoof prints often just the size of one of the pads on Alfred's foot. But the magnificence of the red deer—more Elk sized for those who are more familiar with them—are truly something. They saw us as we left the yard, paused and watched us, then picked up their pace and disappeared. That moment of recognition— acknowledgement?—between species is very special to me and a truly blessed way to begin the morning.

Thank you for being here with me.

Much love,
Susie
xx

Away to the Westward I'm longing to be,
where beauties of Heaven unfold by the sea,
where the sweet purple heather blooms
fragrant and free,
on a hilltop high above the Dark Island.
- Dark Island traditional Scottish Song

THE ART OF AN ENVELOPE

Even before moving to The Gardeners Cottage I had always loved to draw on my envelopes. Why should the pleasure of reaching a letter only start when you open it? Why not send a potential moment of imperfect joy or a smile to everyone that touched the letters as they make their way around the world? The wonderful woman at my local post office would often caress the pile while she checked to "see what you have done" this month before dropping them into the post bag. I hope their whimsy adds some joy to your experience as well.

May: View across Loch Fyne.

June: Sweet peas.

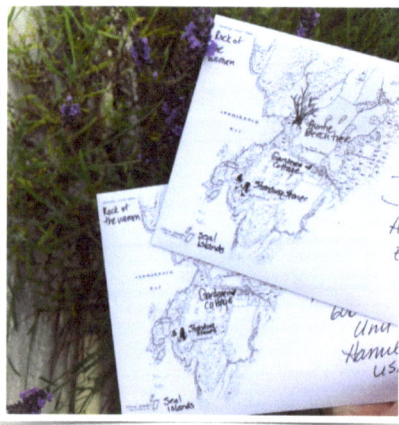

July: Overlay on an ancient map.

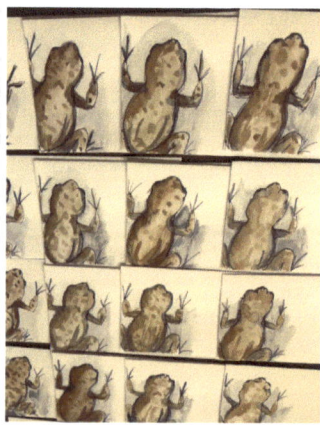

August: Toads!

September: Alfred.

October: Inspired by
paper cuttings.

November: Pheasant.

WINTER GREETINGS

December was this incredible artwork used and reprinted with permission
by Winona Cookie. You can visit her shop to purchase at
https://www.redbubble.com/people/winonacookie/shop

January: Woodpecker

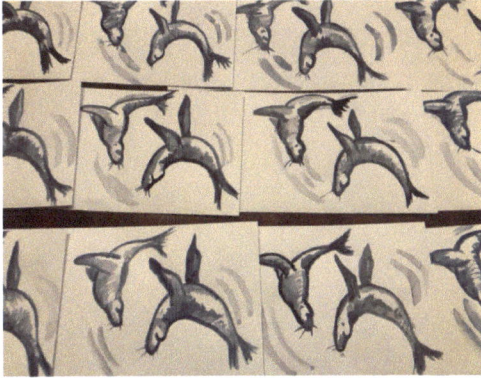
February: Seals

March: Crocuses

April: Standing Stone

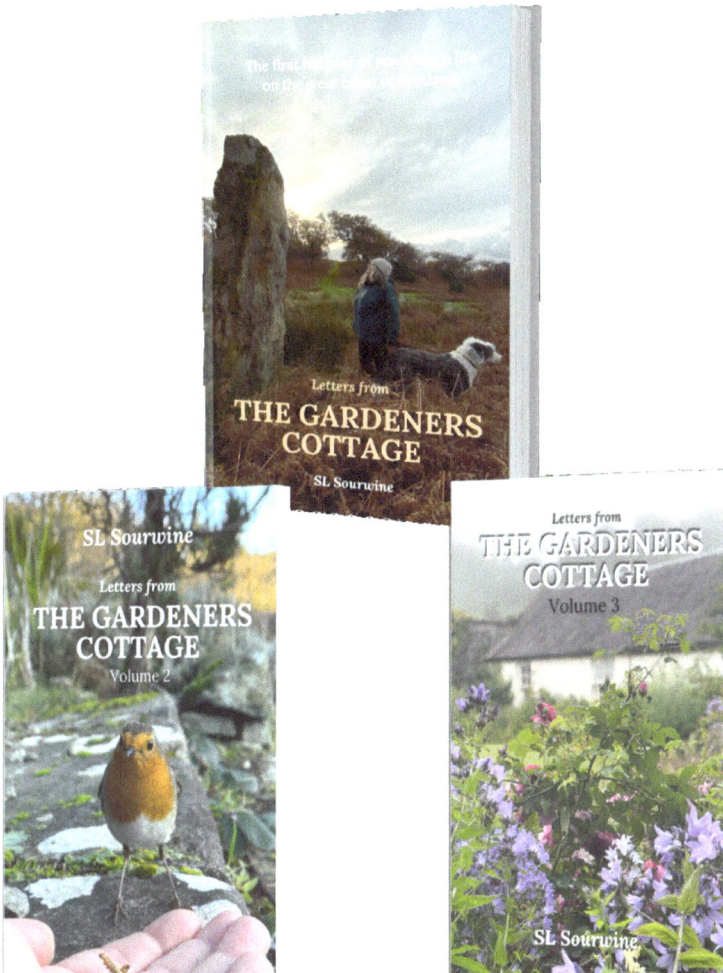

Make sure you have the complete set!

All three years of letters are now available in book and ebook form wherever books are sold online or direct from the website:

SLSourwine.com

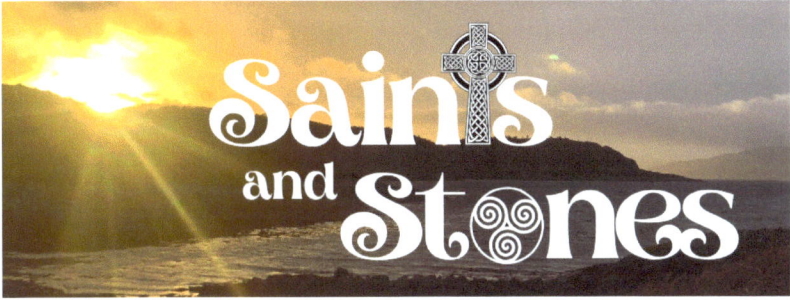

Want more of ancient Scotland inspired by the landscape around The Gardeners Cottage? Subscribe to my newsletter and be a part of the process of the novel coming to life in real time.

History, archeology, dreaming, landscape, myth, and mystics are all inserting themselves in the weaving of these tales. Expect rabbit holes of research, shared chapter drafts, character profiles, research learnings, some artwork that can be part of my creative process, maybe interviews, podcasts and random virtual events.

https://saintsandstones.substack.com/